HERTFO
TALES OF ⊥кY
AND MURDER

Betty Puttick

COUNTRYSIDE BOOKS
Newbury, Berkshire

First published 2001
© Betty Puttick 2001

COUNTRYSIDE BOOKS
3 Catherine Road
Newbury, Berkshire

To view our complete range of books,
please visit us at
www.countrysidebooks.co.uk

ISBN 1 85306 704 0

Produced through MRM Associates Ltd., Reading
Printed by J. W. Arrowsmith Ltd., Bristol

Contents

Acknowledgements

I should like to thank the many people who helped me with my enquiries, particularly the staff of St Albans, Watford, Hoddesdon and Berkhamsted libraries, the *Herts Advertiser* and *Herts Mercury* newspapers, Bishops Stortford Tourist Office, W. Wright, Curator of Bishops Stortford Local History Museum, Dr Paul G. Neeson, Deputy Principal of Berkhamsted Collegiate School, Ann Wheeler, Curator of St Albans City Museum, Cecilia Blaney, Steve Sampson, Paradise Wildlife Park, and Chris Standen, Broxbourne Council animal warden.

INTRODUCTION

When I began to write this book, I was surprised to find how many 'firsts' we have in this county.

First of all, of course, is our saint, Alban, the first Christian martyr. There is mysterious Royston Cave, unique in this country, a bottle-shaped underground cavity excavated in the chalk where two ancient roads cross, its walls carved with crude figures of saints, kings and queens. What was its purpose, and who created it?

Many of Hertfordshire's crimes have excited interest far beyond county boundaries. John Tawell, dignified and respectable in his Quaker garb, had a shameful secret which finally led him to murder. When he left his dying mistress to escape on the train for London, his fate was already being sealed as the police were, for the first time, able to send a message on the new electric telegraph to alert the police at Paddington to his arrival.

And who can forget Graham Young, the serial poisoner, whose ambition was to secure himself a place in Madame Tussaud's Chamber of Horrors? At his trial for poisoning members of his family he was only 14 years 9 months old. And that was just the beginning! When Graham embarked on his next saga of murder after his release from Broadmoor, police were able to prove that a cremated victim had been poisoned by examination of the ashes, a first at the time.

Teenager Ann Noblett went missing one winter evening in 1957, but it was a month before her body was found in woodland. This was one of the most unusual and bizarre murders ever, as her body was frozen solid and appeared to have been kept since her disappearance in a deep freeze, but despite every effort, the mystery of what happened to Ann has never been solved.

Mary Ansell, found guilty of the murder of her insane sister Caroline, who died after eating a cake laced with rat poison, is remembered as the only woman to be hanged at St Albans.

And who was Juliana Berners? Was she a 15th century nun of Sopwell who became the first woman sports writer? Did she, in fact, ever exist?

Every summer a phenomenon shows itself in fields of grain, when overnight increasingly elaborate crop circles appear like magic. Despite the hoaxers who sometimes claim the credit, some designs seem too complex and beautiful to have been created by human hands, unwitnessed and at such speed. Hertfordshire unfortunately can boast few crop circles of any kind, and yet every book or article written on the subject invariably mentions our county. The reason is that in 1678 a pamphlet headed *Strange News out of Hartfordshire* told the story of what experts claim as the very first crop circle, the work of the Devil himself!

These are just some of the stories from Hertfordshire's rich and unusual history of crimes and strange and mysterious happenings, and there are many more. I hope you will enjoy reading about them.

Betty Puttick

THE KILLING OF
WILLIAM WEARE

They cut his throat from ear to ear,
His brains they battered in,
His name was Mr William Weare
He lived at Lyons Inn.
(*Contemporary Broadsheet*)

The John Thurtell/William Weare murder case was one of the outstanding events in the 19th century criminal calendar and evoked enormous publicity and interest because of the colourful characters involved and their way of life in the shady world of gambling, prize fighting and dubious criminal activities.

William Weare was one of the slickest card sharpers in London, who made himself a good living by introducing naïve young gentlemen up from the country to the delights of gambling and, with a skill born of long practice, relieving them of their cash. He was well known at race meetings and boxing matches everywhere and from time to time he had crossed the path of John Thurtell.

Thurtell, too, loved the sporting life. Field sports, horse racing and the boxing ring meant a great deal more to him than the business of silk merchant that he had taken on to please his wealthy father, the Mayor of Norwich. He was an organiser of prize fights and a compulsive gambler, and it was his ambition to become a real swell in the sporting circles he frequented, but although the fights he promoted attracted the crowds, he was generally only a jump ahead of his many creditors.

Some of his prize fighting activities were mentioned by George Borrow in *Lavengro*, and his pen portrait of Thurtell described him as nearly six feet tall, with close cropped hair, a pale, pockmarked skin and lean athletic build, having something of the appearance of a bruiser but with a suggestion of someone performing a role rather than the real thing.

The delights of 19th century London were an obvious magnet to Thurtell. By night the flamboyant gambling dens of the West End teemed with life and huge sums of money were risked in games of chance, and many rued the day they met a certain dapper little ex-waiter with a practised dexterity at both billiards and cards. William Weare knew his way around. The world of gambling, racing and prize fights was his world, but he considered himself a cut above the seedy hangers-on and petty villains who claimed his acquaintance. His black beard was elegantly cut, he wore a well-tailored blue coat with gilt buttons, and he was fussy about his clean collar and wristbands. He had something of a reputation as a blackmailer and informer. Certainly a man to treat with respect.

Thurtell's Norwich creditors were becoming pressing, and he came up to town to collect some money owing to his silk business in order to settle his debts.

He returned home to Norwich with a black eye and an unconvincing story of having been viciously robbed, which his creditors insisted was a ruse to deprive them of their money.

His business and reputation gone, Thurtell thought it prudent to return to London with his brother Tom, where they took on the management of the Black Boy pub in Long Acre, but the place soon acquired a doubtful reputation and lost its licence. The brothers' next venture was the Cock Inn in the Haymarket, another haunt of the hard drinking and gambling fraternity. Then, in another attempt to recoup their finances, the brothers borrowed money to stock a warehouse with silks and other materials and, after insuring it, the premises were completely gutted by fire in January 1823. The County Fire Office, suspecting arson, disputed liability but the Thurtells surprisingly won their case. But before they could get their hands on the money, the insurance company brought an indictment against them for conspiracy to defraud.

Their financial situation was becoming desperate and they were forced to decamp from the Cock Inn, through unpaid debts. It was at this crucial turn in their affairs that William Weare returned to town following the St Leger race meeting at Doncaster, very chipper with his considerable spoils. John Thurtell had been acquainted with Weare for some time, having often met him at Wadesmill in Hertfordshire where they and their like were wont to go for the training of pugilists and an evening or two's gambling. Thurtell had frequently lost a game to Weare's superior skill, and at this low ebb in his own financial situation he must have recalled with some interest that William Weare had no trust in banks. It was said that he preferred to carry his wealth, sometimes as much as £2,000, on his person, and had a special pocket fitted inside his shirt for the purpose.

Among John Thurtell's cronies was one Joseph Hunt, a born loser, who, after a short and inglorious career as landlord of a tavern, was occasionally employed as a singer in the Vauxhall Gardens and other places of entertainment. He had introduced Thurtell to William Probert, a plausible rogue, who had married a wealthy brewer's daughter and subsequently became a wine merchant. His debts had soon made him bankrupt, and after a spell in prison, Probert had rented a small country cottage at Gill's Hill Lane, Radlett, where he ran a jigger, or illicit still.

During a fortuitous meeting with William Weare in a billiard saloon, the idea of a nice little weekend's shooting at Probert's Hertfordshire cottage was suggested. Weare accepted with pleasure and it was arranged that Thurtell would pick him up on Friday, 24th October 1823.

On the Friday morning, Thurtell and Hunt bought a pair of pocket pistols at a pawn shop, and a sack and some rope from a dealers near Westminster Bridge, and discussed certain arrangements that boded no good at all for William Weare.

At about half-past five Thurtell in his black gig met Weare at Tyburn turnpike, Hunt and Probert following close behind, but at Cricklewood they overtook Thurtell's gig. There was obviously time for a little refreshment, and from the Bald Faced Stag inn at Hendon it was brandies and water all the way for Hunt and Probert. By the time they reached the Artichoke at Elstree there was no sign of the gig, but Hunt was confident that he was in plenty of time for his appointment with Thurtell.

But Thurtell and Weare were there first and, finding no accomplice waiting, Thurtell drove rapidly round the narrow lanes and back again. Where was Hunt? Weare sensed that something was wrong and, becoming uneasy, he began to ask questions. Thurtell decided it was now or never, he would have to do the job alone. He pulled out his pistol and fired, but clumsy with nervousness he only succeeded in hitting Weare a glancing blow on the cheek.

Terrified, the little card sharper jumped from the gig and began to stumble up the dark lane, shouting for mercy. But Thurtell leapt to silence him, and as the two men grappled together, rolling over and over in the muddy lane, Weare fought like a tiger for his life. Small as he was, Weare was strong and wiry and it was all the powerful Thurtell could do to get the better of him till, grasping his pocket knife, he struck deep into Weare's jugular vein.

At last, groaning horribly, the little man's grip slackened

and he fell back, his life ebbing away. Sick and exhausted, Thurtell made sure of him by jamming the butt of his pistol hard into Weare's head, then dragging the body into the cover of the hedge he groped in the dark for the money and Weare's gold watch and chain. But in his haste to get away, he forgot his own knife and pistol.

The events of that night were like a macabre Whitehall farce. When Thurtell, Hunt and Probert finally met at the cottage, Mrs Probert and her sister were waiting for their weekend visitors. After a sociable supper with the ladies, Hunt even entertained them with a few songs, including the unlikely choice of *All's Well*, and Thurtell generously presented his hostess with Weare's gold watch chain.

Soon afterwards the ladies went to bed, but Mrs Probert felt uneasy. She knew her William and the company he kept, and hearing the men go out again she watched from her bedroom window. She saw them return leading a horse, and then something heavy in a sack was dragged to the fish pond in the garden. Hearing them come back indoors, she crept downstairs and listened to them apparently sharing out some money.

Financially it had been disappointing, according to Thurtell. There was only six pounds each, but Hunt and Probert knew better than to voice their suspicions.

At first light Thurtell and Hunt went in search of the knife and pistol, but to their chagrin two labourers were repairing the road. Explaining that they had dropped a knife from their gig, Thurtell and Hunt made a perfunctory search but found nothing. But soon after they had gone the labourers were more successful. The knife and pistol, both bloodstained, were found and the workmen also noticed bloodstains on the grass verge beside a damaged hedge.

Thurtell and Hunt returned to London, but back in the country things were beginning to hum. Very little of Friday night's happenings had passed unnoticed in that quiet corner of Hertfordshire. A black gig with an unusual white faced horse had been seen by several people as it careered madly round the lanes, and an Aldenham farmer and his wife had heard carriage wheels, then a shot and groans, but the lady had been too frightened to let her husband investigate. The cloud of witnesses grew, and while Thurtell counted the rest of the money, and Hunt admired himself in Weare's clothes, others were putting two and two together and making what looked suspiciously like a case of murder. But where was the body?

Equipped with a spade and bringing a joint of beef for dinner, Thurtell and Hunt returned to Probert's cottage on the Sunday. They intended to bury the body during the night, but the dogs barked so much that they thought someone must be about. Probert was jittery, insisting that the body must be removed from his pond, and next night while Hunt kept Mrs Probert talking, Probert and Thurtell heaved the sack and its gruesome contents into the gig. Heavily weighted with stones, the body of William Weare finally sank into the depths of a pond near Elstree known as Hill Slough, and Thurtell and Hunt hurried back to London.

But time was running out. Probert was arrested and word was soon on the way to Bow Street to arrest Hunt and Thurtell. Thurtell denied everything despite bloodstained clothing being found at his lodgings, but while being questioned about a pistol found in his possession, he was confronted with its companion with blood and hair adhering to it, which had been found in the lane, and his pallor and obvious shock told their own story. The body had still not been found, but when Hunt was questioned, to save his own skin, he revealed where the body was hidden and it was retrieved and taken to the Artichoke public house.

At the inquest Hunt denied having any part in the murder, although he had to admit to having bought the sack and cord used for the body, insisting that he thought it was for transporting game. And although he had disclosed where the body had been hidden, he denied that he had any part in putting it there. Probert denied knowing Weare, or having ever seen him, insisting repeatedly on his total innocence until the Coroner warned him to say no more.

John Thurtell was charged with the murder, and Hunt and Probert as his accomplices. Before the trial, the case evoked enormous publicity in the newspapers and a spate of books, pamphlets and broadsheet ballads poured from the presses, amounting to the first 'trial by newspaper' and necessitating a postponement of the real trial because the irresponsible publicity might prejudice the jury. There was even a play entitled *The Gamblers* which enacted the whole story, using the identical chaise in which the murder was committed, with the same white faced horse in view, but Thurtell's lawyers had performances stopped, although they were immediately resumed after the trial.

The trial took place on 6th January, 1824 at Hertford, and so much interest had been aroused that vast crowds converged upon the little country town. Every available inn and lodging was full to overflowing and by 4 am on the morning of the trial a drunken, noisy crowd had assembled outside the court house.

It was decided to omit Probert from the indictment so that he could turn King's evidence, and also so that Mrs Probert's vital evidence could be given, which could not have been used against Thurtell if her husband were also charged.

Forty-four witnesses were heard, including the Proberts, and although Mrs Probert became hysterical her evidence was damning.

Thurtell had spent hours preparing a lengthy speech to the jury, much of which he had learned by heart and rehearsed in jail to the admiration of his fellow prisoners. He continued to maintain his innocence throughout but when, after an absence of only twenty minutes, the jury brought in a verdict of 'Guilty', his composure was quite unruffled.

Hunt, convicted as an accessory before the fact, burst into

Penny pamphlets such as these (on view in St Albans City Library) gave all the lurid details of the crime.

a paroxysm of wild sobbing, but Thurtell with amazing sang-froid took an unhurried pinch of snuff, then shaking hands with a nearby acquaintance said 'God bless you, remember me to all friends' and left the court.

The London newspapers used horse expresses in relays to rush the latest news of the trial to London, and lurid details of the vice-ridden underworld poured off the presses. Jemmy Catnach's series of execution broadsheets sold so well that he was reported to have made £500 in pennies from the crime.

Until his execution Thurtell kept calm and all who saw him were impressed by his courageous acceptance of the inevitable. His execution was to be at noon on 9th January 1824, Hunt's sentence having been commuted to transportation for life. As the time for the execution drew near, the press of people in front of the scaffold numbered around 15,000 and many fainted in the crush.

Precisely at twelve a murmur ran round the crowd signalling the prisoner's arrival, and instinctively many present took off their hats. Thurtell bowed in a dignified way to friends and acquaintances in the crowd, then shook hands with the governor and chaplain. The prison governor, clasping Thurtell's hand with deep emotion, exclaimed 'Thurtell, God Almighty bless you' and the prisoner replied 'God bless you, sir'.

Conspirators in murder: William Probert (left) gave King's evidence against Thurtell (centre) who was hanged, and Hunt, transported to Australia.

'Mug shots' from a newspaper at the time of the trial. (Courtesy of St Albans City Library)

It was over very quickly. A new type of gallows was used which acted with merciful speed, and George Borrow, who had known Thurtell for many years, wrote afterwards, 'Why, when his neck broke, it went off like a pistol.'

But that was not quite the end for John Thurtell. His body was taken to Barts Hospital where, before a vast audience, for some weeks the famous surgeon, Mr Abernethy, publicly dissected the body. By the end, the atmosphere had become extremely offensive but, undeterred, thousands visited John Thurtell's gruesome lying in state.

Probert, who left the court a free man, was to follow Thurtell to the scaffold within a year, for horse stealing. Hunt was transported to New South Wales. Some reports say that the boat in which he sailed was shipwrecked, with the loss of all on board, but other accounts say that Hunt eventually made good.

THE DOUBLE LIFE
OF JOHN TAWELL

One cold January day in 1845 an incredible rumour was spreading through Berkhamsted. 'It can't be true — they must have the wrong man!' was the general reaction. 'How could a respectable man like Mr Tawell do a thing like that?' asked the local residents as they hurried to pass on the news that a young woman had been found murdered at Salt Hill, Slough and that John Tawell had been arrested; dignified, well-to-do John Tawell who lived at the Red House!

Although he had not lived in Berkhamsted very long, his many philanthropic activities and interest in education had made John Tawell in his sober Quaker garb a familiar figure in the town, and he and his gentle Quaker wife lived a life of such quiet respectability and benevolence that their association with crime of any kind seemed unbelievable.

The murdered woman was Sarah Hart who lived in a tiny terraced cottage in Slough with her two small children. She had told her neighbours that her husband was abroad, but that she received a regular allowance from his father, a member of the Society of Friends.

It was nearly 7 o'clock on the evening of New Year's Day 1845 when Mrs Mary Ann Ashlee heard stifled screams coming from next door. In the four small terraced cottages known as Bath Place, Slough, there wasn't much privacy

The Red House in Berkhamsted, former home of John Tawell.

and she knew that her neighbour Sarah had a visitor. She thought she had heard raised voices, and then as she listened, she could hear a sort of moaning noise, interspersed with muffled screams. Mary Ann snatched up a candle and set off down her garden path to see what was the matter.

At the same moment the door of Sarah's cottage opened and a man came out. He and Mary Ann reached the gate at the same time and the man fumbled hurriedly with the catch, trying to open it. She recognised the elderly man in Quaker dress as the visitor she had seen arrive earlier, and thought this must be the gentleman Sarah was expecting who brought her quarterly allowance.

'What is the matter with my neighbour? Is she ill?' asked Mary Ann. The man seemed confused and agitated and made no reply, but brushed past her, and as she reached Sarah's door she turned to see him looking back at her. Suddenly afraid, Mary Ann shut the door quickly and bolted it behind her. Then she gasped at the sight which met her eyes. Sarah Hart was a pretty woman in her thirties, kind hearted and friendly with her neighbours, but now she lay sprawled on the floor of her small room, her clothes torn and dishevelled and her long hair unpinned and hanging round a face Mary Ann hardly recognised.

Sarah's eyes were fixed and staring as she gasped painfully for breath. Mary Ann fell on her knees and tried to raise Sarah's head but the sick woman couldn't speak. Quickly unbolting the door, she ran to fetch Mrs Burrett, another neighbour, who offered Sarah some water but she was unable to drink it. They dabbed her head with cold water but it was obvious that Sarah was almost past human aid. They sent for Dr Champneys, who came at once, but he could barely detect a pulse before she died. On a small table by the fire stood an open bottle of porter and two glasses, one still containing some porter. The doctor sent for the constable, who when he heard about Sarah's visitor decided to try and intercept him at the station.

But by the time a messenger reached the station the visitor was in a first class carriage and the 7.45 for Paddington was just leaving. His sober, respectable appearance was daunting, but nevertheless the Superintendent at Slough Station tapped out a message on the electric telegraph to Paddington Station advising the Great Western Railway police officer to follow the Quaker arriving on the train and find out his identity.

When the train arrived at Paddington at 8.20, William Williams, the police officer, was waiting. Seeing the Quaker board a bus, Williams snatched up an overcoat to hide his uniform and hopped up at the back with the conductor. He even took the suspect's 6d fare to the City of London!

At the Bank, the Quaker alighted and disappeared into the Jerusalem Coffee House. Later, still shadowed by Williams, he set off over London Bridge to Scotts Yard, where he went into a lodging house and the vigilant Williams kept watch until it was obvious his man was there for the night.

Did John Tawell sleep well that night? In killing Sarah Hart he had ended the shameful secret life that had threatened his security for so long. He was proud of his position, and his imposing house in Berkhamsted with six servants, a fine carriage and horses, a fitting home for his gentle Quaker wife and their baby son. Surely a man of substance like himself was above suspicion? Any uneasy doubts on his mind were answered quite soon.

By next morning information about the murder had arrived from Slough, and Williams with another officer arrived at the lodging house in Scotts Yard. Tawell had already left, so they went to the Jerusalem Coffee House where they found him and took him into custody. 'You must be mistaken in the identity. My station in life places me above suspicion!' Tawell assured them.

Despite his protest, he was taken to Slough and placed in the custody of Mr Perkins, Superintendent of Eton Police. Tawell at first denied that he had ever been to Slough before, or knew anyone living there. But during dinner that night he mentioned Sarah Hart. 'That wretched unfortunate woman once lived in my service for nearly two and a half years,' he said. 'You didn't know that, did you Perkins? She left me about five years ago. She was a good servant when she lived with me, but since then she has often sent to me for money.' Perkins cautioned him to mind what he said as it could be used in evidence, but Tawell went on. 'I was pestered with letters from her. She was a bad woman. She said she would make away with herself if I didn't give her money. When I went to her house and told her I wouldn't give her any more, she threatened to do for herself. She held a small phial over her glass of stout and said, "I will, I will." Then she poured something out of the phial into the glass and drank it. She lay down on the rug, but I walked out. I certainly shouldn't have left her if I had thought she had been in earnest.'

At the inquest neighbours and tradesmen gave evidence that Sarah was in need of money, and pawn tickets and unpaid bills were found in the cottage. She had lived there for nearly two years and told neighbours that Tawell, who visited her at regular intervals, was her father-in-law. She referred to him as Mr Talbot and said that when she was in his service she had married his son against his family's wishes. Now her husband had gone abroad, but she was allowed to keep the children and lived on an allowance of £1 a month paid quarterly.

At the post mortem the body was found to be healthy with no marks of violence. But when the contents of the stomach were analysed, sufficient prussic acid was found to explain Sarah Hart's unnatural death.

John Tawell, who had pointed out that he was a man of 'some importance' and attending the inquest was 'a serious interruption' for him, now heard the verdict of wilful murder given against him, and by the time he left in a carriage for Aylesbury Gaol, a hostile crowd had gathered and it took nine or ten policemen to get him away safely.

But at Berkhamsted where the news spread like wildfire, people still thought the police must have the wrong man. Poor Sarah Tawell set off at once to see John, never doubting his innocence. They had been married for about four years and had an eighteen month old son. She had been Sarah Cutforth, a Quaker widow, running a high class school for young ladies, but she gladly gave it up when John asked her to be his wife.

They lived comfortably and were happy together. It was true that the Society of Friends had expelled John from their fellowship, and expelled her too when she married him. But the Tawells still used the Quaker form of speech and wore the sombre Quaker garb.

John Tawell's trial took place at Aylesbury in March 1845 and excited great interest. There was practically a pitched battle to get seats on the first day as everyone wanted to see this prosperous Quaker who was supposed to have poisoned his mistress. They saw a slight, grey haired man, about 5 ft 6 ins tall with a thin, intelligent face and a quick, alert manner. He was 61, and had a slight squint in his left eye. So this was the wealthy philanthropist who lived in affluent comfort with his Quaker wife at Berkhamsted, and kept a mistress and her brood at Slough? John Tawell had been a chemist, later a druggist's traveller. As a young man his life was already taking a dual course — outwardly a respectable member of the Society of Friends, he dabbled in forgery, then a capital offence. When he was caught trying to pass a forged cheque at the Quaker bank in Uxbridge, the well-known Quaker aversion to taking life saved his neck. He was sentenced to 14 years transportation and sent to Sydney.

However, in Australia he impressed the authorities by his good behaviour and intelligence and he was granted a ticket of leave after only three years. He soon had his own chemist's shop in Sydney and lucky speculations made him prosperous. He married and came home to England with his first wife, two sons and a daughter.

Here Mrs Tawell became ill, and Sarah Hart joined the household to nurse her. A few weeks later she died, and after his arrest for murder, rumours hinted that Mrs Tawell may have been her husband's first victim, but there was no real evidence of this.

Sarah stayed on, taking over the duties of the mistress of the house. She may have cherished hopes of becoming the second Mrs Tawell, but when John thought of remarrying, it was Sarah Cutforth he had in mind, and Sarah Hart, already pregnant, was given a weekly allowance and hidden away in lodgings in London. Her second child was born there before Tawell decided to move her to a more obscure neighbourhood, in fact Sarah and her children made several moves before they settled in the tiny cottage in Slough.

The medical evidence at Tawell's trial in March 1845 was lengthy as neither the surgeons or chemists involved had any practical experience of prussic acid poisoning, but it was established that $7/10$ ths of a grain of pure prussic acid was enough to destroy life, and there was more than a grain in Sarah Hart's stomach. Metropolitan police enquiries had traced a chemist from Bishopsgate who gave evidence that on the day of the murder, the prisoner came to his shop asking for two drachms of Scheele's prussic acid to treat his ulcerated varicose veins. He had brought an empty bottle with a glass stopper, but as the stopper was stuck he was given the acid in another bottle. He returned next morning saying he had lost the first bottle, and bought two more drachms for fourpence, which he took away in the bottle he had originally brought.

A friend of Sarah Hart's gave evidence that after Mr Tawell's visit last September, Sarah had been violently sick all night. Prosecuting counsel suggested that this may have been an earlier murder attempt by the prisoner.

Defence counsel Kelly harangued the jury eloquently for more than four hours. He was scathing about the medical evidence, and as Sarah had been eating apples before she died, he suggested that the prussic acid could have come from apple pips. This flight of fancy earned him the nickname of 'Apple Pip Kelly'.

With tears in his eyes Kelly read out a letter from Sarah Tawell to her husband, beginning 'My only loved one' and ending 'The year has opened with a lovely day. I hope it is an omen of the future which awaits us.'

'Could any man after receiving such a letter commit an act which would make his wife a widow?' demanded Kelly.

Despite the evidence against him, Tawell remained confident, chatting to friends during breaks and sustaining himself with sandwiches and sherry.

When on the third morning of the trial the Judge began his summing up, it was apparent what he expected the verdict to be. Sarah Hart's stomach had contained a fatal quantity of prussic acid. It was for the jury to decide whether the poison had been administered by John Tawell or by the deceased herself. Whether or not John Tawell had bought the prussic acid to treat his varicose veins, as he had told the chemist, it was clear that on the day Sarah Hart was poisoned he had poison in his possession and on the following day he had not.

The jury were out for nearly an hour, while the prisoner grew pale and restless. When they returned the foreman, in a loud emphatic tone, pronounced one word — 'Guilty' — and sentence of death was passed.

Loyal to the last, Sarah Tawell went to the parlour of the prison governor's house to comfort her John. An eyewitness described him as a 'poor, insignificant little man in his Quaker garb, paralysed with grief.'

Although it was spring, there was snow on the ground when they hanged John Tawell. A strong wind blew driving sleet into the faces of a large crowd in Aylesbury market place as they looked up at the slight figure swinging helplessly like a marionette.

Tawell had left a written statement. It was too late now for anything but the truth, and he openly confessed to the murder of Sarah Hart, and a previous unsuccessful attempt in September. Her very existence had become a constant threat to him, and the only solution he could see was to kill her. So, confident that the respectable façade he had established would place him above suspicion, John Tawell tried to destroy his secret life with four pennyworth of prussic acid, and was himself destroyed.

ROYSTON'S MYSTERIOUS CAVE

Walking along Melbourn Street, Royston, you could easily miss the unobtrusive entrance to a place quite unique in this country whose use and origin are still something of a mystery.

Opposite the newspaper office that was once the Rose and Crown public house, a narrow gap leads to a courtyard where an old green door opens onto steep stone steps. A long tunnel ends in a curious bell-shaped cave roughly 25 ft 6 ins high cut out of the chalk, crowned with a grille in the pavement above. Step into this small circular place and in the light of a single lantern placed high above you are suddenly surrounded by a pageant of primitive carved figures of kings, queens, warriors and saints, the crucifixion and the Holy Sepulchre, also pagan symbols including an earth goddess or *sheela-na-gig*. It is easy to recognise St Christopher, staff in hand, with the child Jesus on his shoulder, St Catherine with her wheel, St Lawrence and others which have been identified as King Richard the Lionheart and his Queen, Berengaria, King David and St George (or possibly St Michael).

It was 1742 when this remarkable cave was rediscovered. Workmen erecting a bench in the butter market struck something hard which proved to be a millstone. This was removed, disclosing a circular shaft about two feet in diameter with foot-holds cut in each side, like the steps of a ladder.

First a boy and then a thin man with a lighted candle were let down the shaft to find a large cavity partly filled with loose earth and rubbish. One can imagine how quickly the news spread round the town and then local people crowded round in great excitement, convinced that buried treasure was about to be unearthed. In the end they so hampered the work of clearing out the soil that it had to be done at night. It must have been quite a difficult job removing so much dirt and rubbish through the opening at the top, and before the cave was completely cleared it was visited by the Rev George North representing the Society of Antiquaries, who reported that among the soil were some decayed bones and a skull, pieces of an earthenware cup and a small piece of brass.

He was followed shortly afterwards by Dr Stukeley, the Society's secretary, who described the cave as 'an agreeable subterranean recess hewn out of pure chalk, of an elegant bell-like or rather mitral form, well turned and exactly circular.' It was Dr Stukeley's theory that the upper part must have been a hermit's cell as the cave was almost beneath the old cross which marked the junction where two ancient roads, the Icknield Way and the Roman Ermine Street, intersect, and it had been the custom from early times to erect a cross at such a place, with often a hermit or recluse living close by to direct travellers and pray for their safety. The cross was known as Roisia's Cross and was traditionally believed to have been erected by Lady Roisia, possibly the wife of Eudo Dapifer, William the Conqueror's steward, and owner of Newsells, the local manor house. Later when a town grew up there it was known as Roisia's Town, which eventually became Royston.

At first the only access to the cave was by way of the narrow shaft, but during a bad winter in 1790 Thomas Watson, a bricklayer who lived nearby, found work for his labourers but cutting a descending passageway 72 feet long through the solid chalk, ending in an arched opening into the bottom of the cave. And enterprising Mr Watson was able to charge the many visitors sixpence a time, including Louis XVIII, at that time an exile in this country.

In 1852 Mr Joseph Beldam and his friend Mr Edmund Nunn, curator of Royston Museum, examined the cave and made a report to the Antiquarian Society, Beldam comparing it to certain ancient caves in chalky land near Gaza and Askelon which were dome or bell shaped. During the Roman occupation the Emperor Severus was in that area and later came to Britain, and remembering that coins and coin moulds of this Emperor were found in the Royston area, Beldam thought it possible that some Roman legion which had been with Severus in Palestine might have played a part in the forming of the Royston cave.

Beldam also suggested another connection with these far-flung caves, which were sited in an area which was one of the battlefields of the early Crusaders. One of Richard I's knights was William de Magnaville, son of Lady Roisia, and Beldam wondered whether he could have created the cave in the style of those he had seen in the Holy Land.

Sylvia Beamon, author of the book *Royston Cave, used by Saints or Sinners*, puts forward the widely accepted theory that the cave was the work of the warrior monks, the Knights Templars, who played an important part in the Crusades. They became a powerful, wealthy and secretive organisation with many connections in Essex and Hertfordshire, including Baldock and Royston.

But the end of the 13th century saw their downfall and persecution. Some Templars were imprisoned in the dungeons of the Chateaux de Chinon in the Loire Valley, where they left carvings similar to those in Royston Cave. Many were executed by burning, but despite the final suppression of the order by Pope Clement V in 1312, some Templars escaped and may have found Royston Cave an ideal place for secret meetings. The saints portrayed in the cave carvings are those revered by the Knights Templars and

Curious carvings underneath Royston. (T. Edmondson, Folkestone, Kent, 71/354, courtesy of Robert Clark)

some of the other carvings have been interpreted as relevant to them such as one said to depict a burning at the stake. There is also a cave in the Ceska Lipa region of the former Czechoslovakia which is similar to the one at Royston, both in shape and carvings.

Crossroads have since ancient times been considered a particularly sacred or magical place and the siting of the cave at the point where the Icknield Way and Ermine Street cross was obviously no accident. The cave remains a mysterious place which stirs the imagination and there may yet be more theories about its use and origin.

In June 2000 there was great concern at the threat to Royston's treasure when it was flooded — water began to rise but fortunately stopped short of the carvings. After so many centuries, it would indeed be tragic if this rare and very strange place should ever be irrevocably damaged.

A PASSIONATE CRIME

O n an April day in 1779 a messenger brought a letter to the young clergyman in the condemned cell at Newgate. It read: 'If the murderer of Miss Ray wishes to live, the man he has most injured will use all his interest to procure his life.' The prisoner knew that the writer, Lord Sandwich, First Lord of the Admiralty, was powerful enough to save him from the gallows, even at this late stage. But the Rev James Hackman had no wish to live. He was fully reconciled to his fate and ready to face the prospect of his imminent execution at Tyburn with composure.

Only days earlier he had played a leading role in one of the most dramatic crimes of the century. The murder of the mistress of the First Lord of the Admiralty on the steps of Covent Garden Opera House by an obscure young clergyman had every element to grip public imagination — passionate love and jealousy and a certain amount of mystery — and indeed the true facts of the relationship between Martha Ray and James Hackman are still not entirely clear.

Martha Ray was born in Elstree in 1746, and at the tender age of thirteen was apprenticed to a milliner in Clerkenwell. But she was scarcely sixteen before her delightful singing voice attracted attention, and she was soon appearing at Covent Garden where a contemporary described her as 'an elegant person, great sweetness of manner and remarkable judgement and execution in vocal

A portrait of Miss Martha Ray.

and instrumental music'. Martha was noticed by Lord Sandwich, then living apart from his mentally unstable wife, and he was sufficiently impressed to take her into his protection immediately, and to organise a suitable education to equip her for a future role as wife in everything but name.

Martha's lovely voice was trained by the best tutors, she learned to play the harpsichord and she was sent to France to acquire the social graces. Lord Sandwich installed her in his home at Hinchingbrooke in Huntingdonshire, where over the years five children were born, brought up and educated as Lord Sandwich's legitimate family.

Martha's warm and agreeable personality brought comfort and happiness to the stormy, controversial politician. He was often unpopular with the public — witness his nickname of Jemmy Twitcher — and even hated for some of his actions, and yet his friends and subordinates found him lovable and a loyal friend. Fanny Burney described him as 'a tall, stout man, looking as furrowed and weatherproof as any sailor in the Navy … he has good nature and joviality marked in every feature'. His way of walking was ungainly, and it amused him to tell a story about how his French dancing master had politely intimated that he would take it as a favour 'if your Lordship would never tell anyone of whom you learned to dance'.

In spite of this, he was undeniably attractive to women, and Martha Ray, although she was so much younger than Lord Sandwich, was very devoted to him, although they had their periods of friction. Martha was extravagant and often ran into debt. Also the fact that she had no real position or security rankled with her, and after their first serious quarrel in 1766 Lord Sandwich was deeply hurt to find Martha was considering taking a professional engagement at Covent Garden. She remarked tartly that since his lordship was finding her 'so expensive' she must do something to help herself. But this quarrel was satisfactorily resolved, and once again, as a friend of the family described it, 'few houses were more pleasant than his — it was filled with rank, beauty and talent, and everyone was at his ease'.

Musical entertainments were a great feature at Hinchingbrooke with Martha in her element, and Sandwich himself was even known to take a hand on the kettledrums, while the guests carolled away merrily.

James Hackman came upon the scene in the winter of 1775. He had entered the Army at 19 and was on a recruiting visit to Huntingdon with a fellow officer who was acquainted with Lord Sandwich. They were invited to dinner at Hinchingbrooke, where the sight of the charming Martha had an immediate effect upon James Hackman. At first sight he was in love, deeply and seriously, with a woman ten years older than himself, the mother of several children and the mistress of one of the most powerful statesmen in the country.

From the first Hackman had serious and honourable intentions towards Martha. He wanted to marry her, but just what her reactions were is not clear. After both were dead a book entitled *Love and Madness* was published, purporting to be a collection of the letters which passed between them, but this apparent evidence of a clandestine affair is considered to be a fabrication on the part of a disreputable clergyman called Croft. Eventually Hackman decided to abandon his Army career and enter the Church, and after he was ordained he obtained a living as Rector of Wiveton in Norfolk. But his time there was brief as shortly after being ordained he went to London, hoping to arrange a meeting with Martha.

He was still obsessed with the hope of marrying her, although on his own declaration in the condemned cell he had not spoken to her since the beginning of 1776, when he had proposed marriage and had been refused. However, through some friends of hers, Senor and Senora Galli, he sent a passionately worded note to Martha at the Admiralty, begging her to see him for five minutes. Martha returned his letter with a short reply, absolutely refusing to meet him and telling him he must give up his pursuit of her as she could have nothing to do with him.

This clear rebuff obviously had a powerful effect on Hackman's already disturbed state of mind. In a letter to his brother-in-law, Frederick Booth, he wrote: 'When this reaches you I shall be no more, but do not let my unhappy fate distress you too much. I strove against it as long as possible, but it now overpowers me. You know where my affections were placed: my having by some means or other lost hers (an idea which I could not support) has driven me to madness. The world will condemn me, but you will pity me. God bless you, my dear F., you were almost my only friend ... May you ever be a stranger to the pangs I now feel. May heaven protect my beloved woman and forgive this act which alone could release me from a world of misery I have long endured. Oh, if it should be in your power to do her any act of friendship, remember your faithful friend J.H.'

It seems that Hackman had decided to shoot himself in front of Martha Ray. On the 7th April 1779 he watched her coach bring her party to Covent Garden, and during the performance he waited in a neighbouring coffee house, drinking brandy and water and keeping an eye on the theatre entrance. He had two pistols with him, ready charged, and as the audience began to filter out of the opera house, he went across the road and joined the crowd.

He saw Martha Ray and her friend Signora Galli come out escorted by Lord Coleraine, and as the linkman called for her coach, Hackman saw another gentleman step forward to offer the smiling Miss Ray his arm. The sight of this possible rival being greeted so charmingly was enough to goad Hackman's already unbalanced brain to action. Pistols in hand he prepared to make an end to his jealousy one way or another. Just as the party prepared to enter the coach Hackman sprang forward, and before anyone realised his purpose he had shot Martha point blank in the head.

She fell dead at his feet, and Hackman then tried to shoot himself, but the glancing shot only wounded him slightly. He, too, fell to the ground, repeatedly hitting his head with the butt of his pistol. They were both carried into the Shakespeare tavern, and after his wound had been treated, Hackman was questioned and sent to Newgate.

Lord Sandwich was at home at the Admiralty, and when the empty coach returned it fell to his old black servant James to bring his master the dreadful news. Lord Sandwich was stunned then ran upstairs and threw himself down on his bed in agony, saying 'Leave me a while to myself. I could have borne anything but this.'

Events moved quickly after this, and the day after the murder a coroner's jury brought a verdict of wilful murder against James Hackman.

On April 14th Martha Ray was buried at Elstree beside her mother, and on April 18th Hackman was tried at the Old Bailey. The court was packed with a fashionable crowd who heard Hackman declare the murder of Miss Ray was not premeditated, he had only meant to kill himself. 'I protest that the will to destroy her who was ever dearer to me than life was never mine until a momentary frenzy overcame me,' he said.

Without retiring the jury found James Hackman guilty and he was sentenced to death. Boswell, who had a taste for trials and their often tragic sequel at Tyburn, attended Hackman's trial while Samuel Johnson and other friends eagerly waited to hear all about it. A heated argument then developed between Johnson and his friend Beauclerk about Hackman having two pistols. Johnson insisted it was proof that he intended to shoot two people, but Beauclerk contended that a man who intended to shoot himself took two pistols to make sure of the job.

After he had recovered from the shock of Martha's death, Lord Sandwich attempted to help Hackman. His friend Captain Walsingham went to Newgate on his behalf, but reported that Hackman was grateful but had no wish to live. He blamed the tragedy on Miss Ray's friend, Signora Galli, who, Hackman said, had told him that Martha had a new admirer. This attempt by Signora Galli to fob off Hackman's unwanted devotion had unwittingly incited the violent emotions which led to the tragedy, and she received a good deal of criticism and ultimately had to leave the stage. When she was in financial difficulties Lord Sandwich helped her with gifts of money.

Hackman met the hangman, the famous Jack Ketch, with composure. For ten minutes he stood in prayer, then dropped his handkerchief as a signal that he was ready. Much to the disgust of the crowd who felt sentimental pity for this young man who had committed so romantic a crime, Ketch kept Hackman waiting while he first picked up the handkerchief before driving off the cart.

Lord Sandwich brought up and educated Martha's children. Two sons, William and John, died young but the eldest boy, Robert, went into the Navy and became an Admiral. Martha's second son, Basil, became an MA, a writer and a distinguished barrister, meriting many columns in the *Dictionary of National Biography*. Augusta, her daughter, became the Countess de Viry.

ST ALBAN'S REPORTER

The young Matthew Paris became a monk at St Albans monastery in 1217 and, succeeding Roger of Wendover in 1236 as the monastic historian, was believed to be the greatest of the mediaeval chroniclers.

At the time St Albans was one of the largest and most powerful monasteries in the country, a hive of activity with a constant influx of important visitors including the King himself. Henry III visited the Abbey many times and he and other great men of the day, passing through on their way to and from London, were an invaluable source of information for Matthew Paris's lively historical chronicle inscribed with a quill pen on parchment.

Besides the important events of his own time, Paris had a journalist's eye for marvels and mysteries. What are we to make of this interesting event in 1254?

'About midnight of the day of our Lord's circumcision, the moon being eight days old and the firmament studded with stars, and the air completely calm, there appeared in the sky, wonderful to relate, the form of a large ship, well-shaped, and of remarkable design and colour.'

Needless to say this attracted the attention of the monks and others who watched the remarkable apparition for a long time. It seemed as if it were really built of planks and painted, but at last it began to disappear, 'wherefore it was believed to have been a cloud, but a wonderful and extraordinary one.'

The gateway to a once large and powerful monastery, St Albans.

In 1257 he records several miracles at the site of Saint Alban's tomb on Saint Alban's day, including two young boys brought back from the dead and others cured of paralysis. Possibly anticipating scepticism, Paris notes that the miracles were proved to be true on the evidence of credible persons. Miracles were attributed to most saints' shrines and tombs in those days; even centuries before, the Venerable Bede in his *Ecclesiastical History* wrote: 'To this day sick people are healed in this place (Alban's tomb) and the working of frequent miracles continues to bring it renown.'

For the year 1249 Paris records a 'freak of nature'. A male child was born, begotten it was said by a demon on the Welsh border. Within half a year his teeth were full grown and he was as tall as a youth of about 17'!

Matthew Paris reports on weather and natural events of

every kind — earthquakes, eclipses, floods, falls of stars and in 1246 a violent hailstorm which lasted for 16 hours with terrible consequences to livestock and birds, and buildings. In 1251 a dreadful storm seemed 'to darken the world' and a thunderbolt crashed through into the Queen's bedroom and crushed the bed to powder. And in December 1236 a second sun was seen beside the real one, which was taken to be an omen of bad weather, followed by storms and serious flooding for two and a half months.

Fearlessly outspoken, Matthew criticised the great and not so good, including the King himself, and even described the Pope's emissaries as 'harpies and bloodsuckers, and plunderers'. He died in 1259, a born historian and gifted writer, leaving behind a fascinating chronicle of the events of his time, great and small.

THE CRIME OF MARY ANSELL

Mary Ansell is remembered as the only woman to be hanged at St Albans Prison. At that time a hundred years ago when the penalty for murder was death there was strong public reaction against the fate of this young servant girl who, although her guilt seemed undeniably proved, appeared too weak minded and immature to be capable of planning such a wicked crime.

Mary had an imbecile sister, Caroline, in Leavesden Asylum, near Watford, and in February 1899 a parcel had arrived for Caroline from her sister Mary containing tea and sugar. When this was used it was found to taste bitter, and so it was thrown away.

Then soon afterwards on 9th March, another parcel arrived which contained a sandwich cake. There was nothing to say who had sent it, but Caroline was delighted and in spite of its rather strange yellow colour, she and other inmates ate the cake, Caroline having most of all. Not long afterwards there was an outbreak of vomiting and stomach pains among those who had shared Caroline's cake, and although everyone else soon recovered, Caroline's condition worsened rapidly and within a few days she died in agony.

It seemed obvious that the unusually yellow cake was responsible, and a post mortem was carried out which showed that Caroline had died from phosphorous poisoning. The police were called in and after hearing about the previous parcel sent by Caroline's sister, they made a search through the rubbish at the asylum and found the cake's wrapping paper which bore a WC1 postmark. The fact that Mary lived and worked as a servant in this area was suspicious, and enquiries then revealed that an insurance agent who called at Mr and Mrs Maloney's house where Mary worked had drawn up a life insurance policy for her for £22 10s 0d on the life of her sister Caroline.

Since Caroline had died within six months of the agreement being signed, the amount due was £11 5s 0d which seemed too small an amount to inspire murder, but it probably meant a year's wages to Mary Ansell.

And Mary was in need of money. Mary had a boyfriend whom she hoped to marry, although he was disappointingly reluctant to agree to Mary's dream of an Easter wedding. In fact, he had made it clear that he considered they should wait until they were better off and could start married life in a suitable home. No doubt Mary thought that money from the insurance policy would change everything, which of course it did.

For the police pursued their enquiries, and a search of her room discovered a jar of phosphorous paste, generally used as rat poison, which a local hardware shop owner remembered Mary buying, telling him that it was to rid the Maloney's house where she worked of rats. However, Mrs Maloney denied any knowledge of this, and insisted that there was no problem with vermin in her house.

Protesting 'I am as innocent a girl as ever was born,' Mary was arrested and appeared at Hertford Assizes on 29th June 1899, accused of the murder of her sister. In court Mary denied having sent either of the parcels to Caroline, and questioned about the insurance policy, she said that she had taken it out so that she could afford to give her sister a decent funeral one day.

Her father was called to the witness box, and presumably did not realise the implication when he said that Mary had pressed him to refuse to allow a post mortem. He said he

A line drawing of Mary Ann Ansell that appeared in the press in June 1899.

thought it was because she could not bear to have this happen to the body of the sister she loved, but Mary herself had admitted that she had not seen or communicated with Caroline since December 1897 when she had sent her a Christmas card. This did not appear to show much sisterly affection, but when reminded that she had told police that she and Caroline were not very good friends, she replied that 'Two better sisters never lived together, so help me God'.

Throughout the trial Mary Ansell exhibited little emotion, as if she was almost unaware of the seriousness of her position. When she was found guilty, the death sentence on this young servant girl brought strong public reaction and many petitions to the Home Secretary were organised in a campaign to have it commuted to a prison sentence, and over 100 members of the House of Commons suggested a postponement of the execution to allow further enquiries to be made into Mary's mental condition. There was even a petition to Queen Victoria but all to no avail.

Was Mary Ansell in her right mind when she sent a poisoned cake to her sister in order to benefit from the insurance policy on her life? Her actions suggest a coldly calculated crime, and yet the strong streak of madness in her family history should have been taken into consideration. All of her aunts had died insane, her employer described her as immature and weak minded, and a doctor

St Albans prison. (Courtesy of St Albans City Museum)

who examined her in prison said she was a 'mental degenerate and ought to be held irresponsible in the eyes of the law'.

Mary Ansell's execution was fixed for 19th July 1899, and her last moments were reported in harrowing detail in the press. Readers were told that in the condemned cell she could hear the hammering as her scaffold was built in the coach house behind the prison gates. Her parents came to say goodbye the evening beforehand, but she expressed no wish to see the boyfriend for whom she had risked so much.

Early on the following morning, a solemn group gathered outside St Albans Prison. Inside the prison Mary was given breakfast, but we are told that, not surprisingly, she ate little. She was clearly overcome and prayed fervently for help. The walk to the gallows was all too short, a mere 30 paces from her cell to where Mr Billington, her executioner, waited to put a hood over her head and the noose round her neck.

No members of the press were allowed to be present although graphic details published regarding Mary's last moments suggests that she was hysterical with fear. But the time had come and as the Chaplain intoned 'Lord have mercy upon us', Mr Billington pulled the lever which dropped Mary Ansell seven feet into eternity. And outside the prison an involuntary gasp went up from the waiting crowd as at two minutes past eight o'clock, a black flag was hoisted from the flagpole.

Mary was buried in the prison grounds, but later when the old prison site became Council property in the 1930s, the four criminals interred there were reburied in the cemetery in Hatfield Road, St Albans.

It is rumoured that some 11 years after Mary Ansell's death, her brother confessed on his death bed to the murder of Caroline. But this may perhaps have been a last minute attempt to clear his sister's name of a crime that, mentally unbalanced or not, she almost certainly committed.

DEATH IN A TEACUP

Many people grow up with a cherished ambition, whether they achieve it or not. Graham Young's dream was to become a famous poisoner, famous enough to secure him a place in Madame Tussaud's Chamber of Horrors! And from an early age he set about his remarkable career as a serial poisoner with single-minded dedication.

Born on 7th September 1947, his mother died when Graham was only three months old, and his father's sister Winnie, who had a small child of her own, took charge of the baby. Graham grew into a happy toddler in the only home he had known, but his father Fred, then a young man of 33, had fallen in love with Molly, an Irish girl who worked with him, and they were married on 1st April 1950. Everything changed for the Young family. Fred was now able to have Graham and the boy's older sister, Winifred, to live with him and his new bride in their house on the North Circular Road, Cricklewood.

On the surface Graham apparently adapted to the change in his life, but later according to classmates he obviously saw Molly in the role of wicked stepmother, and his relationship with his father had always lacked warmth and affection. He found it difficult to form friendships with children of his own age and spent more and more time in the library, where he borrowed everything he could find on medical science, crime, black magic, war and Nazism.

An early clue to his developing interests came when his

DEATH IN A TEACUP

45

stepmother found a hole in the pocket of Graham's school coat, apparently caused by a half-empty bottle of acid. He'd found it in the dustbin of a Neasden chemist's shop, he said. Molly spoke to the chemist, and also to the librarian who was reassuring about Graham's rather macabre taste in literature. But Graham's obsession with Hitler and the war caused friction with his father, and when Molly regularly checked his pockets after the acid episode, it was a shock one day to discover a wax model stuck with pins.

Poisons and famous poisoners were of obsessive interest to him, and from books he learned about the symptoms and effects of different poisons. One day he went to a chemist's shop in Neasden and asked for 25 grams of antimony, managing to convince the chemist that he was 17, the minimum legal age for buying restricted poisons. He was at the time only 13½, and inspired by this first success, he continued to buy more antimony, giving a false name and address when he signed the poison register.

Classmates of his at that time said Graham always kept a small phial of this poison with him and liked to pass what he called his 'little friend' round among the boys. One friend, Chris Williams, remembered how Graham, jealous when he became more friendly with another boy, challenged him to a fight. Graham lost, and angrily threatened 'I'll kill you for that'.

Soon afterwards Chris became sick during afternoon school and had to go home. The same thing happened the following week, and he realised later that each time Graham had shared some sandwiches with him at lunchtime. But at the time Chris had no suspicion. When the two boys went to the zoo one Saturday Graham brought along some lemonade and, after drinking it, Chris became violently sick and was ill for several days but his doctor found nothing specifically wrong.

It was at about this time that Graham's stepmother Molly found a poison bottle containing antimony in Graham's room, and visited the chemist to make sure no more poison was sold to the boy.

In 1961 Molly, Graham's father Fred and sister Winifred all suffered bilious attacks one day and suspected a tummy bug. No one thought that Graham could have anything to do with it, especially as he, too, was sick one evening while visiting his Aunt Winnie.

Aunt Winnie, who had looked after Graham as a baby, at first thought his family's mysterious illnesses could be due to lead pipe poisoning, or a contaminated water supply, but although she had always been fond of Graham, she began to wonder if her nephew might be responsible.

Molly continued to suffer stomach trouble, and one morning after Graham's sister Winifred complained that her tea tasted sour, she was taken ill on her way to work. During the day she felt dizzy and was unable to focus properly, and at Middlesex Hospital, after tests, she was told that she appeared to be suffering from belladonna poisoning.

Winifred blamed Graham who, she thought, had obviously been careless with one of his experiments, but her accusations apparently distressed him so much that Winifred apologised. However, unknown to his family, 14 year old Graham had by now acquired a stock of antimony, atropine, arsenic, digitalis, aconite and thallium!

Meanwhile Molly was getting no better, but despite hospital tests, no reason for her symptoms was discovered. But on Easter Sunday 1962 she woke with pins and needles in her hands and feet and a stiff neck and became so ill that she was taken to Willesden Hospital where she was kept in for observation. But in the late afternoon, just as she was insisting she must go home, Molly suddenly died. At a post mortem, Molly's death was attributed to a spinal injury, possibly due to a bus crash she had been in the previous year.

After Molly's cremation, people felt sorry for Graham, who had lost both his own mother and now his stepmother too. Fred, depressed after Molly's death, had another really bad attack of sickness, diarrhoea and stomach pains soon after the funeral and was sent to hospital. He was soon home again but later had to return and this time tests indicated that he appeared to be suffering from arsenic or antimony poisoning. Graham showed great interest, knowledgeably discussing the difference between the two poisons with the doctor. It proved to be antimony poisoning, and Fred was told that any more of it would have been fatal. As it was, his liver was damaged.

Aunt Winnie eventually asked Graham outright if he had poisoned his father. He was deeply hurt at the suggestion and indeed it seemed inconceivable that a boy of Graham's age could do such a thing.

But one man thought otherwise. Graham's science master who, impressed by the boy's knowledge, had encouraged him to use the laboratory, was becoming increasingly concerned about Graham's experiments. In his desk the teacher found bottles of poisons, essays about famous poisoners and some of Graham's macabre drawings of dying people. He and the head teacher visited the Youngs' doctor who told them about the family's succession of illnesses.

Before going to the police, they arranged for Graham to be seen by a psychiatrist, giving him the impression that he was seeing a careers officer. Graham was only too pleased to show off his knowledge of poisons and describe his experiments and went home convinced that a brilliant university career lay ahead of him. The psychiatrist went to the police.

Next day a Detective Inspector called and inspected Graham's room where he found quantities of various poisons. He went round to Aunt Winnie's house where Graham was staying and told her the boy would be arrested for the malicious administration of poison.

Graham arrived from school, quite unconcerned at the sight of the police. His pockets contained nothing unusual, but inside his shirt police found his 'little friend', the phial

Graham Young in 1962, aged 14, at his first trial.

of antimony, and two other bottles containing thallium. At the police station Graham at first denied everything. But next day, he confessed what he had done and revealed various hiding places where he had secreted poisons. He was charged with poisoning his friend Chris, his father and sister and remanded for trial at the Old Bailey where he appeared on 6th July 1962 and pleaded guilty to all three charges. He was 14 years, 9 months old.

In his statement read out in court he said, 'I have been interested in poisons, their properties and effects since I was about eleven,' and described how he put a few grains of poison on food which he gave to his friend Chris, and members of his family.

'By September of last year', he said, 'this had become an obsession with me. I knew that the doses I was giving were not fatal, but I knew I was doing wrong. It grew on me like a drug habit, except it was not me who was taking the drugs. I realise how stupid I have been with these poisons. I knew it all along, but I could not stop it.'

At the trial, the prosecuting counsel said that poisoning had nothing to do with Molly Young's death, which had been due to natural causes. Later, Graham would confess to Aunt Winnie that the night before Molly died, he had given her twenty grains of thallium in her evening meal — enough to kill twenty people.

The senior medical officer at the Ashford remand centre, Dr Christopher Fysh, gave his view that Graham was suffering from a psychopathic disorder, not mental illness, and should go to a maximum security hospital such as Broadmoor. Dr Donald Blair, a consultant psychiatrist who had examined Graham at Ashford, said he appeared to feel no ill will towards his victims, they just happened to be near at hand for his experiments in drugs and their effects. In his opinion, Graham Young presented a very serious danger to other people, and Mr Justice Melford Stevenson committed him to Broadmoor for a period of fifteen years, not to be released without the express authority of the Home Secretary.

Young arrived at Broadmoor in July 1962. Books on the Nazis and medical textbooks were still his favourite reading, and he enjoyed giving his fellow inmates his impersonation of Hitler. After three years, he made his first application for release, but at the tribunal his father was adamant that his son should never be released, and the application failed.

Disappointed, Graham's old habits reasserted themselves. An empty packet of sugar soap was noticed on the lower shelf of the tea trolley and the urn was found to contain the contents of the packet, which would have had dire consequences for any tea drinker.

A spell in the maximum security rooms after this escapade taught Graham that if he was to have any hope of an early release, he could not afford this kind of behaviour.

The hospital superintendent Dr McGrath and the senior psychiatrist Dr Udwin took a close interest in Graham Young and the possibility of his early release. In June 1970 Udwin encouraged him to hope, and reported to the Home Office that in his opinion he was no longer a danger to others.

Graham's sister Winifred, now married and living in Hemel Hempstead, was asked if she would be willing to have him to stay for a few days. Winifred was naturally concerned for the safety of her new baby, but reassured by Udwin, she and her husband Dennis collected Graham for a week's holiday on 21st November 1970. All went well and Udwin, delighted at the successful outcome, arranged with Winifred that Graham should spend Christmas with them.

Graham enjoyed Christmas enormously and couldn't wait for his eventual release. He resented having to return to Broadmoor, and told one nurse, 'When I get out, I'm going to kill one person for every year I've spent in this place.'

Was this intended as a sick joke? Who knows. His boast that he intended to go down in history as the most famous poisoner since Crippen had often been made during his time in Broadmoor, but after years of close observation and regular psychological tests Doctors Udwin and McGrath sent a recommendation for release to the Home Office. It was signed and the release date was fixed for February 1971. In preparation for getting a job, Graham took a course in store-keeping at the Government Training Centre at Slough where he made friends with another trainee, Trevor Sparkes, a friendship Sparkes would deeply regret. Young often invited Sparkes to his hostel room for a glass of wine but Sparkes developed sickness and stomach pains, and was so ill he had to spend four days in the training centre's sick bay. Later he felt well enough to play football, but had to leave the field when he seemed to be losing control of his legs.

At the end of their training at the centre, Young offered Sparkes something to 'calm his nerves' before a job interview, but instead he became violently sick and, after seeing his doctor, he was sent to hospital at Welwyn Garden City where a possible strain was diagnosed.

In April 1971 Young was interviewed for a vacancy for a storeman at John Hadland Ltd of Bovingdon, manufacturers of optical and photographic instruments. He had an excellent reference from the Government Training Centre and, asked about his previous experience, said he had suffered a nervous breakdown after his mother's death in a car accident and had needed mental treatment, but was now completely better.

Hadland's contacted the training centre regarding Young's psychiatric treatment and were given Dr Udwin's report, which they found satisfactory. Graham got the job, to start work on Monday 10th May, and moved into a bedsitter in Hemel Hempstead, neither the house owners or his new employers having any inkling of his past, as it was not the policy of the probation service to disclose such information.

The photographic plant of John Hadland Ltd at Bovingdon where Young poisoned several of his workmates, two fatally.

In the meantime he visited the chemists, John Bell and Croyden in London and asked for 25 grams of antimony potassium tartrate. He produced an authorisation headed 'Bedford College, London' and the chemist assumed he was a medical student. Young signed the poison register giving a false name and address. The staff at Hadland's found Young rather an odd character, often moody and withdrawn, but always ready to discuss politics, Hitler and, of course, chemistry. But Bob Egle, 59, in charge of the storeroom, part-timer Frederick Biggs, 60, and Jethro Batt, 39, who sometimes gave Young a lift home, welcomed the newcomer. And Young in turn tried to be helpful, and each day when the tea lady wheeled her trolley along the corridor, leaving it to each department to collect their own mugs of tea, he volunteered for this duty.

On 3rd June, Bob Egle went home suffering from

diarrhoea, but by 7th June he was back at work. The next day another employee, Ron Hewitt, also developed stomach trouble and sickness, and he, too, had to go home. His doctor suggested some kind of food poisoning, but although he came back to work, the trouble kept recurring. Bob Egle took a week's holiday and returned feeling better. But his recovery was shortlived. By the next day his fingers became numb, and later at home in bed his back was very painful and his feet, too, became numb. His doctor sent him to Hemel Hempstead hospital, and later, after transfer to intensive care at St Albans City Hospital, his condition deteriorated rapidly and on 7th July he died. After a post mortem, death was given as due to paralysis which affected his respiratory muscles — later found to be consistent with the large dose of thallium he had been given.

Young accompanied the managing director to the funeral, and in the car, discussing the cause of Mr Egle's death, he impressed Mr Foster with his medical knowledge. Young had often talked to Mr Egle about his war experiences and remarked, 'It's very sad that Bob should have come through the terrors of Dunkirk, only to fall victim to some strange virus.'

Early in September, the saga of illness among the staff recurred when Fred Biggs developed sickness and stomach pains, but he was due to go on holiday and returned on 20th September, as fit as usual. But on the same day Peter Buck, the firm's import-export manager, became violently sick after having a cup of tea with Young and had to be taken home.

On 8th October, David Tilsen felt sick after his tea break, and woke next morning with pins and needles in his feet and numbness in his legs. A few days later Young had a curious conversation with Jethro Batt, describing how easy it could be to poison someone and get away with it.

He offered Jethro a cup of coffee, but when Jethro found it too bitter to drink, Young laughingly asked if he thought he was trying to poison him. Minutes later, Jethro was violently sick and went home.

That weekend Batt's legs and stomach were painful, and unknown to him his colleague Tilson now had chest pains and was having difficulty breathing. After admittance to St Albans City Hospital, Tilson improved slightly, but his hair began to fall out.

At Hadland's, Mrs Diana Smart, who sometimes worked in the storeroom, felt ill after drinking a cup of coffee with Young and went home to bed.

Batt, at home in great pain, was hallucinating and his hair had begun to fall out. He was admitted to hospital.

Tilson went home from St Albans Hospital on 28th October, but had to be re-admitted on 1st November. Normally a man with a thick head of hair and a beard, his doctor now described him as like a 'half plucked chicken'.

With several workers away, Fred Biggs and his wife came in to help Young, who made sure everyone had plenty of cups of tea. Next day Fred developed chest and leg pains and was admitted to hospital on 4th November, and later transferred to a London hospital.

As, one by one, fellow workers suffered similar alarming symptoms Hadland's was buzzing with rumour and conjecture. Was the water supply contaminated or could recent radioactive work on the disused airfield nearby be the problem? Not surprisingly, Graham Young's apparent immunity caused comment, and he was not pleased to find that Diana Smart was suggesting he could be a carrier of some kind of disease. Poor Diana soon paid for her remark when later that day she became ill again and had to go home.

Dr Robert Hynd, Hemel Hempstead's Medical Officer of Health, was called in and he and a medical team examined the premises and questioned staff, but the cause of the alarming outbreak of illness remained a mystery.

Poor Fred Biggs' condition remained very serious, the

cause unidentified, and after he was moved to the National Hospital for Nervous Diseases, he died on 19th November.

Morale was now very low among the staff at Hadland's and a local GP was asked to try to calm their fears. Dr Anderson assured them that there was no possibility of radiation poisoning from the old airfield. It was true also that heavy metal poisoning had been suggested, but thallium used industrially in the manufacture of high refractive index lenses was not in use at Hadland's and could be ruled out. The remaining possibility, he said, was a virus of an unusually virulent kind, and everything was being done to identify it. Had anyone any questions?

Graham Young apparently had. He described heavy metal poisoning and its effects and pointed out how similar these were to the symptoms experienced by Hadland's staff. Anxious not to arouse even more concern among the workforce, John Hadland closed the meeting. He and Dr Anderson now shared suspicions, and Hadland spoke to Detective Inspector John Kirkpatrick at Hemel Hempstead police station who came over and realised from the employment register that there could be a link between Graham Young's arrival and the outbreak of illness.

Fate then took an extraordinary turn. Detective Chief Superintendent Richard Harvey, head of Hertfordshire CID, was attending a luncheon in London for forensic scientists when Kirkpatrick phoned him. Harvey described the mysterious illnesses at Hadland's to two fellow guests who promptly diagnosed thallium poisoning. He returned to Hertfordshire and he and Kirkpatrick had an urgent discussion with John Hadland. Full details about Young had now been received from Scotland Yard and he was arrested at his father's house in Sheerness.

Meanwhile, police entering Young's Hemel Hempstead bedsitter had been stunned by what they found. In a room papered with pictures of Hitler and other Nazis there were innumerable bottles and other containers with chemists' labels, and on a chair was a pile of crude drawings of graves, tombstones, skulls and crossbones, grotesque figures wielding hyperdermic syringes and poison bottles, some bald or with hair falling out. And, most significant of all, on the floor by the bed the police found what proved to be a detailed poisoner's diary.

Taken back to Hemel Hempstead, Young was told that the police were making enquiries into the death of Frederick Biggs.

Harvey had read the diary found in Young's room, but when he asked him to identify the people referred to by initials, Young claimed that they were all figments of his imagination. But next day he said he had used sodium tartrate mixed with antimony salt on Di Smart, thallium on Bob Egle, Fred Biggs, Jethro Batt and David Tilson, and antimony potassium tartrate on Peter Buck, Ron Hewitt and Trevor Sparkes. Harvey asked him why he had done it, when he had no reason to feel enmity towards any of these people.

The chilling reply was: 'I suppose I had ceased to see them as people. They became guinea pigs.'

At the Metropolitan Police Forensic Science Laboratories, traces of thallium poisoning were found in Frederick Biggs' organs and Graham Young was charged with his murder and remanded in custody.

Permission was sought to exhume the ashes of Robert Egle and proof of thallium poisoning was found. Young was also charged with Egle's murder, the first time in criminal history that a murder charge had followed the exhumation of cremated ashes. He was also formally charged with causing grievous bodily harm to Diana Smart, Peter Buck, Ronald Hewitt and Trevor Sparkes by the administration of poison.

Young was committed on 22nd March at Hemel Hempstead for trial. He had decided to plead 'Not Guilty', and looked forward to a long trial with plenty of publicity. Young's solicitor, John Pickworth, had difficulty in persuading a QC to take the case but at last Sir Arthur

Graham Young took this picture of himself in a photo booth at Waterloo Station and distributed it widely at the time of his 1972 trial.

Irvine, was retained and the trial was fixed for 19th July 1972 at St Albans Crown Court.

A high spot of the trial came when Mr John Leonard QC, for the prosecution, read from the chillingly methodical diary of Young's murderous activities at Hadland's. He had written, 'If it looks like I will be detected then I shall have to destroy myself,' but in fact, when arrested, he had no opportunity to use his 'exit dose'. During the trial, Young continued to insist that the diary was a work of fiction. He said he would certainly not have left it lying around if he had thought anyone would take it seriously.

And as witness after witness told their story and the damning evidence mounted, he continued to present a cool, confident façade, denying everything and dismissing his confession to Harvey as a 'mere convenience' to curtail the police interrogation and get the clothing, food and sleep he wanted. 'I had little doubt the statements would be disproved by subsequent analysis,' he said.

Under the incisive questioning of the prosecuting counsel, his replies were clear and articulate. It was an impressive performance; Young standing, hand in pocket, in his immaculate black suit, apparently fully in command of the situation. When his macabre drawings were exhibited to the jury and the court, Young was unfazed, repeating again that they were a symbolic representation of scenes from a possible work of fiction.

In his defence, Young's QC, Sir Arthur Irvine, referred to Young's habit of showing off his medical knowledge, suggesting that it would be extraordinary for a guilty man to risk revealing such knowledge if he wanted to conceal murder. Final speeches on both sides were fairly short and the jury were out for just over an hour. While waiting, Young told his warders that when sentenced, he would commit suicide by breaking his neck on the rail of the dock. But when the time came, the extra warders there to restrain him were not required. There were no histrionics.

He was found guilty of murdering Egle and Biggs, attempting to murder Batt and Tilson and guilty of administering poison to Hewitt and Mrs Smart. Sir Arthur Irvine then gave the court details of Young's previous record, and said that he saw it as his duty to his client to point out that Graham Young was only able to commit these offences because he had been released on licence from Broadmoor. 'This release may appear to have been a serious error of judgement,' he said, 'but the authorities had a duty to protect Young from himself as well as a duty to protect the public.'

He went on to say that if his Lordship was balancing the desirability of a custodial sentence against a hospital order, Young himself considered that prison would be better for him than a return to Broadmoor. And in view of the tragic consequences of 'the Broadmoor experience', he suggested that his Lordship might think a prison sentence was preferable.

His Lordship Mr Justice Eveleigh agreed, and Young was sentenced to life imprisonment on two counts of murder and two of attempted murder, and five years imprisonment on each count of administering poison to Mrs Smart and Ronald Hewitt. He was taken to Parkhurst maximum security prison on the Isle of Wight where in August 1990, just before his 43rd birthday, he died, reportedly of a heart attack.

No one can deny that Graham Young fulfilled his ambition to join the ranks of famous poisoners, both in the history of crime and in Madame Tussaud's and Anthony Holden's book *The St Albans Poisoner* inspired a film, *The Young Poisoner's Handbook*.

Somehow the fact that his murderous activities were done apparently in a spirit of impersonal research makes his crimes all the more chilling. Graham Young's story is unforgettable and, one hopes, unique.

THE MYSTERY OF THE
ALIEN BIG CATS

It is forty years now since reports were being received of the unlikely sighting in the Surrey countryside of what appeared to be a very large cat indeed. It was said to be about the size of a large labrador, golden brown in colour, with a cat-like face and a black stripe down its back. The usual experts were quick to suggest that the deluded witnesses had obviously seen a large dog, a fox or a feral cat, but the increasing number of people, including police, who had had what was sometimes an uncomfortably close view of the creature, knew that what they had seen, however unlikely, was a puma!

What became known as the Surrey Puma was only the beginning. The sightings of animals entirely out of place in the British countryside spread to other parts of the country, particularly the West Country, soon famous for the Beast of Bodmin and/or the Beast of Exmoor, and it was now evident from reports, photographs and videos that as well as the lynx-like golden brown variety of Big Cat, there were also black panthers on the loose.

The mystery was compounded by the fact that the animals seemed to come and go with almost supernatural elusiveness, and none were ever caught.

Despite the efforts of farmers, who were losing livestock to the marauders, and of huntsmen, police and volunteers of every kind, attempts to catch the creatures were unsuccessful. Some suggested that what had actually been seen was the legendary Black Dog, Black Shuck, known throughout the country as a terrifying supernatural creature with blazing eyes. And although there were still people who considered the mysterious Big Cats to be in the same league as UFOs and the Loch Ness Monster, the number of sightings seemed to prove that they were real enough.

But where did they come from?

It is generally believed that they originated from animals which escaped or were released after the introduction of the Dangerous Animals Act in 1976 which meant that such creatures had to be kept safely in enclosures. It is also thought likely that some Big Cats are still kept illegally, and if they escape they are not, of course, reported as lost.

From the early sightings of the Surrey Puma, to the beasts now roaming nationwide, what of our own local countryside with its more usual wildlife population of squirrels, muntjac deer, rabbits, badgers and foxes? Are there larger predators slinking, mainly unseen, through our own woodlands and commons?

Well yes, actually! There is the Hoddesdon lynx for a start, and the Beast of Barnet or the Monster of the M25, and the Much Hadham puma! Read on!

In August 1998 two East Herts police officers driving into the car park by Bramfield Park Woods at 11 pm noticed what they thought were the eyes of a fox reflected in the car's headlights. The animal drew near enough for them to realise that it was bigger than a fox. It was about the size of a labrador dog, but as it turned to run away, they realised that it was a Big Cat.

It seems likely that it was the same creature which disturbed the sleep of a couple in Braughing the previous night. They woke to hear an alarming low growling sound outside and found their pet cat sitting on the bedroom windowsill, apparently stiff with fright. Next morning revealed some clumps of fur and claw marks in the garden.

What became known as the Hoddesdon lynx was seen prowling in the grounds of Sheredes Junior School, Hoddesdon in May 1998. Earlier in the week some parents had seen a large cat-like animal apparently stalking muntjac deer which were drinking from a stream at the back of the school. It seemed such an unlikely sight that they were embarrassed to report it, but the next day the school caretaker also noticed a similar animal in the same place, and after two teachers saw a lynx-like creature about the size of a labrador with a cat-like face and tufty ears pacing along the edge of the playground, the police searched the nearby wood. The children were escorted home and the school closed next day as a precaution.

Broxbourne Council's animal warden, Chris Standen, installed a large dog trap at the school, baited with a leg of lamb kindly donated by Sainsbury's, hoping to catch the animal. I asked him if he thought it was a lynx, and he agreed. He said he had a good view of it from about 25 yards away as it walked up and down on the fence above the tennis court at the school. But despite the lure of the lamb, the lynx kept a cautious distance although afterwards it was seen several times by parents and children attending the school.

A Hoddesdon woman spotted a mysterious animal in a field about a mile from the school. It was about three to four feet long, darkish brown, with a dark face and a head roughly the size of a football. Earlier in the month several of her chickens had been killed and she wondered if the lynx had been responsible.

In September 1998 at South Mimms, about 9 miles from Hoddesdon, there were two sightings of a sandy coloured cat-like creature with a black ring on the tip of its tail, near the junction of the A1 and M25, and the following day a similar animal was seen at South Mimms by two policemen,

The 1998 sightings of the Hoddesdon lynx featured in many newspapers.

and others, and also in Potters Bar. Pawprints about 3–4 inches in size were discovered, and local residents were advised to keep doors and windows closed, and on no account approach the 'puma-like creature'.

Helicopters with thermal imaging cameras went in search, also teams of police, RSPCA and representatives from London Zoo, and there were a number of reported sightings of the Beast of Barnet or the Monster of the M25 before it apparently departed for pastures new. Subsequently a woman walking near Gobions Wood, Brookmans Park saw a large cat-like creature on two occasions. She was convinced it was not a domestic cat, and described it as larger than a Great Dane dog. It was on the edge of a field and moved away fast as she approached.

Another Brookmans Park resident accompanied a police tracker on a walk round Gobions Wood after seeing an animal disappear into the undergrowth when he was out with his dog. He said it was much larger than a dog, but its movements were cat-like. The tracker was convinced that there were several of what appeared to be pumas in the area near Brookmans Park, probably living on rabbits, foxes and badgers, but despite several sightings in recent years, no one has managed to obtain a photograph or any evidence other than paw-prints.

In November 1999 the owner of a riding club at Much Hadham saw an animal lying by the hedge which leapt up and ran off as she approached. 'It was jet black and about the size of a small alsation dog,' she said. 'But I knew it wasn't a dog because of the way it arched its back as it leapt.' She had heard an animal screaming a few days before, and found the leg of a muntjac deer in her riding arena later.

Police wildlife liaison officers generally advise that there is no evidence that these alien creatures are a threat to humans so long as they are not harmed or threatened. So what should you do if you find yourself looking into the eyes of a Big Cat? Expert advice is: Don't turn your back and run. Slowly back away, maintaining eye contact, and if you have a dog with you, put it on the lead immediately. A dog's instinct may be to attack and it could be seriously hurt, but if you have the dog close at hand, the puma or panther will keep away unless threatened. Many witnesses have found that a Big Cat instinctively makes off on unexpectedly encountering a person.

These animals' stealth and speed may leave a witness wondering just what it was they thought they saw, particularly at night, and reports of a lion on the loose are most likely to be a sighting of a brown or sandy coated puma, also known as a cougar or mountain lion. There was even a sighting of what was described as a tiger by a man riding his motor cycle across Northchurch Common in April 1999. He rode past it unmolested and reported it to the police, but neither Whipsnade or Woburn Safari Park reported any tiger missing, and there were no other sightings in the area.

Animal keepers at Paradise Wildlife Park compare a cast of the lynx's pawprint with the paw of a captive wolf: 'It's big ... nearly the size of a human hand.' (Photo courtesy of Margaret Goodchild)

News of Big Cat sightings during the year 2000 seemed to have tailed off, although not everyone reports what is still an unusual happening. But in early May 2001 there were signs that the Broxbourne area had not heard the last of its exotic visitor. A local resident found unusually large pawprints by the pond in their garden which backs onto woodland in Wormley West End. A cast was taken of one of the pawprints and Steve Sampson, Director of Broxbourne's Paradise Wildlife Park, confirmed 'It is a lynx. It's big — the paw is nearly the size of a human hand.'

And a local resident who owns a domesticated wolf was in Broxbourne Woods during the early May Bank holiday, and his pet was obviously showing signs that it was aware of something frightening. Anyone owning a lynx, a dangerous wild animal, must be licensed, but Broxbourne Council say that none are registered in private ownership in the district.

Gobions Wood, where several Big Cat sightings have been reported.

So if you go down to the woods today remember that, as the song says, there may be a big surprise. When I was in Gobions Wood last May all I saw was bluebells — but you never know — there seems to be something unusual in the Hertfordshire woodland, and it's not a teddy bear's picnic!

THE DEEP FREEZE MURDER

Murders that despite every effort remain unsolved are never forgotten. So perhaps one day the mystery of what happened to teenager Ann Noblett on a dark winter evening in 1957 will at last be unravelled.

It was Monday afternoon, 30th December when Ann, who lived at Marshalls Heath Lane, Wheathampstead, met two girl friends and went to a dancing class at Lourdes Hall, Harpenden. They left around 5.30 pm and walked down Southdown Road to Station Road where Ann had planned to catch the No. 391 bus home, but it was just moving off and as she had missed it Ann said she would walk along to Church Green and catch another bus there.

There seems some uncertainty about which bus Ann caught but she was next seen just after 6 pm by a poultry girl, Shirley Edwards, employed by her father, near the junction of Luton Road and Marshalls Heath Lane and they called 'Hello' to each other. Shirley Edwards noticed that a bus was pulling away from Cherry Tree corner at the time. She had just ridden down Marshalls Heath Lane on her scooter and said later that she had not passed anyone in the lane or seen any parked cars. And that was the last known sighting of Ann Noblett alive.

Ann's home where she lived with her parents was about half a mile down the narrow, quiet lane. When I visited the area while researching this book, I could see that Marshalls Heath Lane has probably not changed much if at all since

Marshalls Heath Lane as it looks today.

1957. There are other houses in the lane, and also premises which have been a pig farm and a variety of other businesses, with Ann's house at the far end. There is still no street lighting along the lane and at just after 6 pm that December evening it must have been quite dark.

When she did not arrive home as expected, naturally her parents were anxious. Ann was a home loving girl with no known boyfriends, who could always be relied upon to let her parents know where she was going, and it would have been completely out of character for her to have gone off somewhere without letting them know. After her parents alerted the police to her disappearance that evening, a widespread search ensued on New Year's Eve 1957 when police with tracker dogs searched surrounding fields and woodland and the River Lea.

As the search widened 300 soldiers and many local volunteers joined in and Ann's description was circulated throughout the area. Ann, who was studying domestic science at Watford Technical College, was a well built girl, 5 ft 8 ins tall, fresh faced with dark hair and wearing two-toned glasses. She was due to become a student nurse at Great Ormond Street Hospital in October and hoped to become a children's nurse. Enquiries revealed that two men had alighted from a 365 bus from Luton to St Albans via Wheathampstead near the Cherry Trees stop a few minutes after Ann Noblett had been seen near there by Shirley Edwards. They stood talking for a few moments before one of them set off up Marshalls Heath Lane, branching off at a footpath leading to the rear of the Lea Valley estate.

He told the police that as he walked along the footpath he noticed two red lights further along the lane which could have been the rear lights of a car, or perhaps a motor cycle combination, or even two bicycles. At the time he had, of course, no reason to take any particular notice of them. He heard nothing, and some other people who were walking down Marshalls Heath Lane a few minutes later also saw and heard nothing.

The search widened and intensified throughout Hertfordshire, and the Essex CID were consulted over the case of a Dutch girl, Marie Kreik, whose body was discovered after she too had recently disappeared from a lonely bus stop, in case there was any connection between the two cases.

Through the local press the Chief Constable of Hertfordshire thanked the many people and local firms that had come forward with help in the search. But not everyone is inspired by the same public spirit and far too often police time is wasted by mischievous telephone calls which must of course be investigated.

Apparently one Luton man made 35 such calls during the investigation, ringing the police with false information and also pestering other people connected with the case. When caught he proved to be a man with a bad record who had already spent some time in Borstal, and his malicious interference earned him a six month prison sentence.

It was a month after Ann Noblett disappeared without trace on her way home that two Whitwell brothers, Hugh Symonds, aged 21, and his 14 year old brother, Brian, took their dog Rip for a run. The dog dived into Youngs Wood, Rose Grove Lane, Whitwell after a rabbit and Hugh followed, and as they entered a clearing they came upon the body of Ann Noblett. They went straight home and telephoned the police.

There had been no attempt to hide the body. It lay about 75 yards into the wood from the nearest field, and about 300 yards from a deeply rutted cart track leading from the Whitwell-Kimpton road. Ann was wearing the same clothes she wore on the day she disappeared, including her glasses and chromium steel wristwatch, and her purse containing thirty shillings lay beside her. But there was something which made this murder one of the most unusual and bizarre in the history of crime. When found Ann Noblett's body was frozen solid and when Home Office pathologist Dr F.E. Camps performed a post mortem, his opinion was that it had been kept in a refrigerator to foil attempts to find out the exact time of death.

Dr Camps told the Coroner that death had been caused by compression on the neck, which did not necessarily mean strangulation, and the girl had been interfered with sexually. The brief inquest was adjourned until April 14th.

Hertfordshire police were joined in the investigation by Scotland Yard detectives, and it was concluded that Ann had been murdered on the night she was reported missing, but her body had then been kept in a deeply frozen condition and had only been brought to the wood not long before it was found. A local press report that police were considering searching local houses and gardens was denied by the police just before the discovery of the body, but this could have triggered the murderer's decision to move it. There were several car tracks going into the wood and police thought she had probably been brought there by car and then carried into the wood, possibly by two people as one person would have had difficulty carrying the body the 300 yards from the road and there were no signs that it had been dragged along the ground.

The place where the body was found was quite isolated and may have been known to the murderer. The wood was a game reserve and the local gamekeeper was able to confirm that although he passed the place most days with his dogs when he came to feed his pheasants, he had seen nothing and if the body had been there his dogs would almost certainly have discovered it.

There was now a new line of enquiry into all the deep freeze equipment within an area of about 30 miles around Whitwell. A reporter making his own enquiries interviewed a poultryman who remembered that while driving home at dinnertime on the previous Thursday (the day before the body was found) he had to pull up onto the grass verge to pass a black Austin car parked on the road some distance from the wood with a well built man sitting inside. It had a Hertfordshire registration 'RUR' but he did not notice the number.

During the adjourned inquest it was said that in the course of the investigation some 2,000 people had been interviewed and many cars checked, and there had been an intensive search throughout the area and over most of Hertfordshire, but up to that time the police had not found sufficient evidence to identify the person or persons responsible for Ann Noblett's murder.

The Coroner recorded that Ann died at some place unknown between 30th December 1957 and 31st January 1958, and had been unlawfully killed by some person or persons unknown.

News of the Mary Kreik case surfaced in 1959 when two men were taken in for questioning in Southend by Essex police, and curiously enough, one of them was a refrigeration expert, but both were later released.

All these years later, the mystery of Ann Noblett's murder has not been solved but Hertfordshire police confirm that it remains an open investigation.

GOING ROUND IN CIRCLES

In the 1970s a strange new phenomenon appeared in the countryside, mainly in Wiltshire and Hampshire, and people were intrigued to find huge flattened circles in fields of grain which turned up overnight, origin unknown. By the 1980s interest was growing fast, and although experts lost no time in producing explanations, ranging from whirlwinds, mating hedgehogs or the earth's magnetic field to visits from alien space ships, the mystery remained.

There was something about the secrecy and speed with which a circle appeared that suggested that we were in the presence of something quite extraordinary, and as time went by, the circles became more and more complex in design, the summers of 1999 and 2000 producing the most amazing complex works of cereal art yet seen.

The fact that a large proportion of the circles have appeared in Wiltshire, well known as UFO country, has added to the feeling that something extraterrestrial may be involved. Were they trying to communicate with us? And who were they? Strange lights were sometimes seen over the fields at night and many who have entered a crop circle have testified to feeling oddly disorientated.

We soon discovered that crop circles were not our exclusive mystery. Similar formations were appearing in Australia, the US, Japan, Russia, New Zealand, Europe, in fact as early as 1974 a Canadian farmer claimed to have seen several shining discs whirling low above his rapeseed crop, leaving behind circles that were approximately the same size as the discs.

As always, there have been plenty of scientists and other experts ready to debunk any over-imaginative ideas, followed in 1991 by two retired Southampton artists, Doug and Dave, who admitted producing hundreds of circles over the past twenty years or so with nothing more elaborate than a plank of wood on a rope. No doubt the early circles could be produced quite easily by hoaxers, and many more claimants followed Doug and Dave, but the exquisitely elaborate pictograms which followed were well beyond their capabilities.

In November 2000 the first crop circle hoaxer to be fined for his handiwork was Matthew Williams who produced a huge seven point star in a Wiltshire wheat field to ridicule people who thought complex shapes must be the work of 'strange forces', but when he admitted his responsibility, he was taken to court. He still insisted that the majority of crop circles were man-made, but grudgingly added 'I do believe some are the work of the paranormal'.

Unfortunately Hertfordshire can boast few crop circles, although a respectably complex one was reported on 18th June 2000 at Cuffley near the railway station. And yet we have a special claim to go down in crop circle history as the site of one of the very first in 1678!

A 17th century pamphlet headed *The Mowing-Devil: Or, Strange News out of Hartfordshire* reads: 'Being a True Relation of a Farmer, who Bargaining with a Poor Mower, about the Cutting Down Three Half Acres of Oats; upon the Mower's asking too much, the Farmer swore, That the Devil should Mow it, rather than He: And so it fell out, that very Night, the Crop of Oats shew'd as if it had been all of a Flame; but next Morning appear'd so neatly Mow'd by the Devil, or some Infernal Spirit, that no Mortal Man was able to do the like. Also, How the Said Oats ly now in

The Mowing-Devil:

Or, *Strange* NEWS out of

Hartford-ſhire.

Being a True Relation of a Farmer, who Bargaining
with a Poor *Mower*, about the Cutting down Three Half
Acres of *Oats*; upon the *Mower*'s asking too much, the *Farmer* ſwore, *That the Devil ſhould Mow it, rather than He*:
And ſo it fell out, that that very Night, the Crop of *Oats*
ſhew'd as if it had been all of a Flame; but next Morning
appear'd ſo neatly Mow'd by the Devil, or ſome Infernal Spirit, that no Mortal Man was able to do the like.
Alſo, How the ſaid *Oats* ly now in the Field, and the Owner
has not Power to fetch them away.

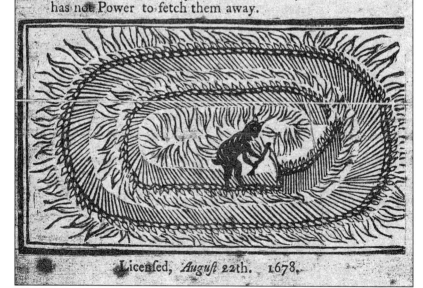

Licenſed, *Auguſt* 22th.   1678.

*The Mowing-Devil — from a 17th century pamphlet in St Albans
City Library.*

the Field, and the Owner has not Power to fetch them away.'

The accompanying woodcut shows the Devil, scythe in hand, cutting the oats in circles, every stalk laid 'with that exactness that it would have taken up above an age for any man to perform what he did that one night. And the man that owns them is as yet afraid to remove them.'

This pamphlet has caused great interest among cerealogists and is almost invariably mentioned in anything written on the subject, although in the pamphlet the Devil is described as cutting the oats whereas in crop circles the stalks of the grain are bent, not cut.

A few hundred years later some may have their doubts about the Devil or any other supernatural force having a hand in the increasingly elaborate designs which appear every summer in our harvest fields, but the phenomenon remains an intriguing mystery, as yet not satisfactorily solved.

JULIANA BERNERS

Who was Juliana Berners? Was she a 15th century prioress of Sopwell Nunnery who emerged surprisingly as our first woman sports writer, or was she an enigma, a literary mystery, a woman who never was?

Early in 1480, three years after William Caxton set up his printing press in Westminster, the third printing press to be established in England was set up at St Albans. Over the next six years eight books were printed, the last one being *The Boke of St Albans* by Dame Juliana Berners or Barnes, containing three treatises on hawking, hunting and coat armour. At that time hawking was a favourite recreation in aristocratic circles and hunting, too, was enjoyed with gusto by all sections of society. *The Boke of St Albans* deals knowledgeably with these sports, and displays a robust approach to the dismembering of animals that is not for the squeamish.

Ten years later, Caxton's successor, Wynkyn de Worde, published a second edition, embellished with delightful woodcuts, adding a further section, 'Fishynge with an Angle'. The book was a big success throughout the 16th century, and its circulation is said to have probably exceeded that of every other contemporary production other than Holy Writ.

But what is known of this nun who was apparently such an expert in field sports? In truth, very little, but lack of adequate information has never deterred her would-be biographers. Born around 1388, she was thought to have been a lady of rank who would have acquired her wide sporting knowledge at Court and, after retiring to a cloistered life at Sopwell, occupied herself by writing her famous *Boke*.

By 1549, Bale, who wrote an account of British celebrities, was describing her as 'an illustrious lady, abundantly gifted in mind and body'. Chauncy, in his *History of Hertfordshire* (1700), presented her with Sir James Berners for a father and by 1810 a new edition of the *Boke* included a full biography: 'Julyans or Juliana Barnes, otherwise Berners, who has been chiefly designated as authoress of the present volume, is supposed to have been born towards the latter end of the 14th century at Roding-Berners in Essex. The received report is that she was the daughter of Sir James Berners, and that she once held the situation of prioress of Sopwell Nunnery in Hertfordshire.'

But by 1888 a facsimile copy was published with an introduction by Wm. Blades, author of *The Life and Typography of Caxton*. Dismissing the 'sham biography', Blades states, 'She probably lived at the beginning of the 15th century and she possibly compiled from existing MSS some rhymes on hunting.'

The section on hunting is the only part of the *Boke* which actually bears the name of 'Dam Julyans Barnes' and Blades contends that the hawking and coat armour sections were evidently compiled from other manuscripts of the time. Literary copyright was still in the future, and a good deal of 'compiling' or plagiarising was not unusual. So what of the original printer? Wynkyn de Worde referred to him as 'the Scolemaster Printer of Seynt Albons' whose first six books were scholastic works in Latin. Then in 1483 came *The Chronicles of England*, a history in English, followed by *The Boke of St Albans* in 1486.

If Juliana Berners was prioress of Sopwell nunnery, surely there are records of the time, but here again we draw a

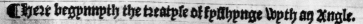

'Fyshynge with an Angle' from 'The Boke of St Albans'.

blank. In 1416 Matilda de Flamstede was prioress, succeeded in 1430 by Letitia Syttenham. Then comes a gap at what should be the crucial time and the next record tells how Joan Chapell was set aside due to age and infirmity in 1480, when Elizabeth Webb then became prioress. So where was Juliana? The *Dictionary of National Biography* quotes from Dugdale's *Monasticon Anglicanum*, ed. 1821: 'It must not be concealed that no such person can be found in any authentic pedigree of the Berners family nor did county historians of Hertfordshire, or indeed any other writers, notice her from documents.'

The few remaining copies of the first edition of *The Boke of St Albans* are, of course, rare and valuable. It seems unlikely that we shall ever know the truth about its author. Was she a real person, this talented and knowledgeable lady obviously well acquainted with the virile pleasures of the hunting field? Or was she — like her book — 'compylit togedr at Seynt Albons', her book an anthology of other works, her name a printer's inspiration? It is significant that in time gone by masters of hunting employed men to look after the horses and hounds who were known as berners! A curious coincidence, or an apt choice of pseudonym?

WHO KILLED SARAH STOUT?

At about six o'clock on a cold March morning in 1699 the body of a young Quaker woman was found caught in the stakes of the Priory mill-dam at Hertford. Her name was Sarah Stout, and at the coroner's inquest later that day it was decided that she had committed suicide while the balance of her mind was disturbed.

One of the chief witnesses at the inquest was Spencer Cowper, a young barrister who was in Hertford for the assizes. He was a member of a prominent Whig family, and his brother William was the Member of Parliament for Hertford. He was well acquainted with the Stouts who were family friends, and he had in fact had dinner and supper at Sarah Stout's home the previous day when he arrived in Hertford. He declared Sarah to be a very modest woman, and said that when he saw her she had not seemed to be particularly troubled, discontented or melancholy, nor yet in love, and there was no reason that he knew why she should have drowned herself. But he was to change his story later when he found himself on trial for her murder.

After the inquest, Spencer Cowper set off for the Essex Assizes, making no attempt to offer his sympathy or assistance to Sarah's bereaved mother, Mary, whose late husband had been a good friend of the Cowpers and given them great support in the parliamentary elections in Hertford.

It throws rather a revealing light on Spencer Cowper's character that his first act on hearing of Sarah's fate had been to send an ostler from his lodgings round to the Stouts' stables to fetch his horse, fearing, he said, lest the coroner's jury might bring in a verdict of *felo-de-se* and the animal might be forfeited to the lord of the manor.

Spencer Cowper's subsequent indictment for murder was

Spencer Cowper

in some quarters considered to be a 'frame-up', prompted on the one hand by the Tory minority in Hertford wishing to discredit a member of a prominent Whig family, and on the other hand by the Quakers. As Spencer Cowper bitterly declared, 'They would rather send four innocent men to the gallows than let it be believed that one who had their light within her had committed suicide.'

And so on 18th July 1699 Spencer Cowper, who was the last person known to have seen Sarah Stout alive, appeared in court on the charge of murder. Also charged were John Marson and Ellis Stephens, attorneys-at-law, and William Rogers, scrivener, who had, like Cowper, been in Hertford that March for the assizes.

An account of what happened on the day Sarah Stout died was given by her maid, Sarah Walker, as her mother, being a Quaker, was unable to take oath and so could not give evidence. Apparently the Stouts were expecting Cowper to stay with them while he was in Hertford as his wife had written to Sarah a few days earlier. He dined with Sarah and her mother and returned again about 9 pm for supper, and sat talking to Sarah, who asked the maid to make a fire in Cowper's bedroom.

Then she told the maid to warm his bed, and while she was busy with this, Sarah Walker heard the outer door close and thought Cowper had gone out with a letter he had been writing. But when she came downstairs both Cowper and her mistress had gone and, at a loss to know where she was, Sarah's mother and the maid sat up all night waiting for her return.

As for the other three accused, their behaviour had aroused suspicion. Two of them had booked lodgings earlier in the day and arrived there between eleven and twelve at night bringing Marson with them to share their room. They asked for a fire and some wine and invited the landlord to have a drink with them. He noticed that Marson's head and feet were very wet, and he was 'all of a reaky sweat'. Marson's explanation was that he had just ridden hard from London, but he had actually been in the town for several hours.

The men began questioning the landlord about Sarah Stout, teasing Marson with being her old sweetheart, but he answered, 'She hath thrown me off, but a friend of mine will be even with her by this time.' Rogers agreed that 'her business was done and Sarah Stout's courting days were over.'

Marson then apparently asked the others how much money they had spent, and was told, 'What's that to you? You have had forty or fifty pounds for your share.' They asked Marson if the business was done, and he said he believed it was, but if not it would be done that night.

When questioned at the trial about this curious conversation, the accused said they had enquired about Sarah Stout in a jesting way as they had heard that a mutual friend had courted her. The rest they denied.

It was a lengthy case with much conflicting evidence in an attempt to decide whether Sarah Stout had drowned or was dead before her body entered the water, but the question of whether her body had floated or not could not be conclusively proved as it had been found entangled among some stakes in the mill-dam in a manner which made it impossible to know whether it was supported by these or not. It was agreed that there was little or no water in her body and this was confirmed by doctors who conducted a post mortem six weeks after her death. Her mother had insisted on this to refute scandalous gossip that suggested that Sarah had been pregnant. There were marks on Sarah's neck and behind her ear which could have been caused by assault and strangulation, but might also have been due to contact with the mill stakes. Her gown was missing when she was discovered and could not be found although the river was well searched several times. But a week before the trial it was found, ragged and torn, hanging on a stake which the miller had cleared of weeds only half an hour before.

No one had seen Sarah Stout since her maid left her sitting in the parlour with Cowper at about half-past ten by the town clock. Cowper said he had left her there after arguing over his decision to sleep at his lodgings rather than at the Stouts' home. He arrived at the Glove and Dolphin inn just as the clock struck eleven and paid a small bill for horse-keep, a trifling matter which could surely have kept until next day — unless, of course, an alibi might be useful. He went on to his lodgings where he was in bed before midnight, and witnesses agreed that he went out no more than night.

At the inquest Cowper had described Sarah as apparently neither troubled, melancholy, nor yet in love, in fact, in no state of mind which might have inspired her to drown herself. But at his trial his attitude changed completely and he called witnesses, including his brother's wife, to describe Sarah's increasing melancholy and threats of suicide, and with a show of reluctance, revealed that she had cherished an unrequited passion for himself, producing two letters to prove it.

The first, dated the previous March 5th, read: 'I am glad you have not quite forgot that there is such a person as I in being, but I am willing to shut my eyes and not see anything that looks like unkindness in you, and rather content myself with what excuses you are pleased to make, than to be inquisitive into what I must not know. I should very readily comply with your proposition of changing the season, if it were in my power to do it, but you know that lies altogether in your own breast: I am sure the winter has been too unpleasant for me to desire the continuance of it. And I wish you were to endure the sharpness of it but for one hour, as I have done for many long nights and days, and then I believe it would move that rocky heart of yours, that can be so thoughtless of me as you are; but if it were designed for that end, to make the summer the more delightful, I wish it may have the effect so far as to continue it to be so too, that the weather may never overcast again: the which if I could be assured of, it would recompense me for all that I have suffered, and make me as easie a creature as I was the first moment I received breath. When you come to H___ pray let your steed guide you, and don't do as you did the last time: and be sure to order your affairs to be here as soon as you can, which cannot be sooner than you will be heartily welcome to your very sincere friend.'

The second letter, dated March 9th, said: 'I writ you by Sunday's post, which I hope you have received: however, as a confirmation I will assure you I know of no inconvenience that can attend your co-habiting with me, unless the grand jury should thereupon find a bill against us, but won't fly for't, for come life, come death, I am resolved never to desert you, therefore according to your appointment, I will expect you, and til then shall only tell you that I am Yours etc.'

But Sarah's mother and brother did not think that the letters were genuine, the writing was not like her usual hand and the style was uncharacteristic.

Sarah Stout had been her late father's main heir, and Spencer Cowper had offered to advise and help her in the management of her financial affairs. He admitted arranging a £200 mortgage for her, the interest on which he paid her the night she died. Also according to a pamphlet published after the trial, both Sarah's mother and a close friend of hers understood that Cowper was arranging the purchase of an estate in ground rents, which he had told Sarah was a very good bargain, and she was intending this for her portion if and when she should marry. Cowper had told Sarah to keep this matter to herself, but she had confided in both her mother and her friend that 'Spencer Cowper had a great deal of her monies in his hands and that he was to have more', and after her death about £1,000 could not be accounted for.

Her mother asked Spencer Cowper in front of the Lord

Chief Justice Holt what money he had in his hands of her daughter's. He answered 'None', and added angrily that he thought his reputation would have held him above suspicion or examinations of that kind.

Apparently he said afterwards that he had demanded proof that he had any of Sarah Stout's money in his hands, but when her mother tried to tell what she knew she was stopped and told she could not speak unless she would swear on oath, which of course being a Quaker she could not do.

At the end of the trial the Judge summed up, declaring that he could not imagine what could induce the accused to commit such a crime, nor yet what could persuade a gentlewoman of plentiful fortune and good reputation to destroy herself, unless her brains had been turned by love. He ended somewhat abruptly: 'I am sensible I have omitted many things, but I am a little faint and cannot repeat any more of the evidence.' Half an hour later the jury returned a verdict of 'Not Guilty'.

Sarah's dissatisfied family tried to arrange a second trial, but the attempt failed due to the influence of the powerful Cowper family. Cowper continued to practise at the Bar, eventually becoming a judge in the Court of Common Pleas, where he showed considerable mercy towards those appearing before him on the charge of murder. He died in 1728 at the age of 59, and in the Cowper mausoleum in Hertingfordbury church there is a memorial by Louis Roubiliac erected by his second wife, showing him in his judge's regalia between the figures of Faith and Justice.

The story of the unbalanced, lovesick girl and the blameless young lawyer is the generally accepted one, but no one can deny that there are loose ends. The trial and published contemporary comment leave the reader with questions that can now never be answered. Who really did kill Sarah Stout?

DEAD RECKONING

Everyone wonders about life after death, and Hertfordshire history records many sceptics who thought they knew just how to prove that they were right. Lady Anne Grimston is rightly or wrongly remembered as one of these.

According to local legend, Lady Anne declared that the possibility that she would rise again to life eternal was just as likely as that a tree would grow from her grave, but that if there was a God, he would cause a tree to grow. Strangely enough, as the people who have visited her grave in Tewin churchyard can testify, since her death in 1717 large ash and sycamore trees have burst from her tomb and made havoc of the iron railings. And the fact that Lady Anne was really a true believer has done nothing to spoil the story over the years.

William Hutchinson who died in 1697 also professed no belief in the possibility of immortality, and his tombstone in Aldenham churchyard was also split into pieces by sycamore trees.

In the graveyard of St Mary's church, Watford, the Fig Tree Tomb was for very many years the great attraction. Master mariner Ben Wangford was buried there in the mid-18th century, after arranging with his relatives that something should be placed with his remains that would grow as a sign that there was an afterlife. Apparently, although Ben didn't give a fig for immortality, fame in the shape of a flourishing fig tree eventually grew from his grave, although sadly it did not survive some particularly bad weather in 1963.

Then there were other Hertfordshire residents who, while not doubting the resurrection, had other post-burial concerns. William Liberty, who died in 1777, visualised a grim free-for-all on Judgement Day as the dead rose up from their graves and in the mêlée he feared he might have difficulty in making sure that he had the right bones! So he was buried in splendid isolation in a field at Flaunden close to the old church ruins.

Fear of being buried alive inspired Robert Orme, a 19th century Rector of Essendon, to leave instructions that his tomb was to be above ground, with a door which could be opened from the inside, the key to be left with his body. He also asked that a loaf of bread and a bottle of wine should be placed in the coffin, and his requests were followed when he died on 23rd October 1843. It was 38 years before it was thought safe to plug the keyhole and seal up the door to his tomb, where he rested beneath an inscription: 'in the hope of a joyful resurrection'.

But one 16th century Braughing man did come perilously close to being buried alive. Farmer Matthew Wall's coffin was being carried down Fleece Lane to St Mary's Church on 2nd October 1561 when it was accidentally dropped and as the bearers stooped to pick it up, they heard vigorous banging from inside. They opened the lid and Matthew sat up, rubbing his eyes.

Back home, he soon recovered and, in fact, the bell that had tolled dolefully for his funeral rang out merrily for his wedding the following spring. He was to live on until 1595, and in his will he left the sexton money for the bells to be rung every year on October 2nd, the anniversary of his lucky escape. This became known as Old Man's Day when first a funeral bell was tolled, quickly followed by a joyful peal of wedding bells.

At Weston churchyard two stones twelve feet apart mark the grave of Hertfordshire's legendary giant, the mighty Jack o'Legs, remembered as a sort of local Robin Hood, a danger to travellers passing along what is still called Jack's Hill at Graveley where he had no trouble relieving them of their money or property.

They say Jack was so tall that he could stand talking to his friends through their first-floor windows, his arms on the sill. He was a friendly, amiable chap, who would frequently help himself to the contents of the local bakers' shops and pass the bread on to poorer neighbours. But at last his light-fingered habits caught up with him, and a party of Baldock men lay in wait for Jack and overpowered him. Told that his hour had come, Jack had one request, that he could shoot an arrow from his bow and that they should bury him where it fell.

The arrow flew straight for Weston church, where it glanced off the tower and fell to the ground where Jack's grave is still marked with two stones. They say that when

Jack o'Legs' grave in Weston churchyard.

visitors used to arrive to marvel at the size of Jack's last resting place, the parish clerks would produce a hefty bone, said to be the giant's thigh bone! Apparently this treasure was bought by famous gardener John Tradescant in the 17th century, passing on eventually to the Ashmolean Museum at Oxford, but its whereabouts today are unknown.

Brent Pelham's ancient church contains an altar tomb let into a recess in the north wall, its marble slab ornamented by a dragon, and an angel carrying a soul to heaven. This is the tomb of another legendary Hertfordshire character, Piers Shonkes the dragon killer, said to have fought and vanquished a mighty dragon which terrorised the neighbourhood. Unfortunately for the brave Shonkes, this dragon was a particular favourite of the Devil's, and in his fury the Evil One declared that when Shonkes died he would have his soul, whether he was buried inside or outside the church... But the Devil was foiled, for Shonkes' tomb was set into the church wall, and so was neither inside or outside.

Piers Shonkes' tomb in the church wall at Brent Pelham.

THE SEARCH FOR JANIE

On the last day of the Easter holidays in 1977 two boys wheeling their bicycles through thick bracken on Nomansland Common on their way home almost stumbled over what looked like a bundle of rags, half buried in sticks and leaves. But as they bent to look, it was frighteningly obvious what they had found, and the two boys aged 10 and 11 rushed home in shock to tell their parents of their alarming discovery.

The police were told, and immediately accompanied the boys and parents back to the Common where it took a little time to again locate the place where the body of a young woman lay almost hidden in the undergrowth. The search for pretty blonde Australian Janie Shepherd, missing since the previous February 4th, was over.

That night Janie had driven her dark blue Mini Cooper from her home in St Johns Wood, London to visit her boyfriend at his flat in Chelsea. She never arrived and was reported missing, and four days later her car was found parked on a yellow line in Elgin Crescent, Notting Hill. It was spattered with chalky mud and with the sunroof slashed, and detectives established that the car had been left where it was found early on the morning of February 5th.

Janie's body was identified by dental records, and the post mortem established that she had been killed by intense pressure on her neck, crushing some of the bones, which suggested a killer of considerable strength.

Janie Shepherd.

One curious aspect of the case was the fact that Janie's body was not dressed in the clothes she was wearing when she left home. She then had on a man's checked shirt, fawn polo neck sweater and a white cardigan with a reindeer motif. When found, she was in a black sweater with red polo neck and green cuffs, which belonged to her and was thought to be part of a change of clothes she probably had with her when she left home.

While police were searching for her missing clothing, a Wheathampstead resident reported that he had noticed some clothes lying at the site of the new school playing field, and later he noticed a man pick them up and walk off. But despite police requests for information, no one came forward and there was, of course, no proof that the clothes were Janie's.

A considerable amount of time had elapsed from when 24 year old Janie went missing to the discovery of her body but a number of people reported possible sightings of her car in the Nomansland area on the night of the murder, and a fruitless search was made for a family who had parked a caravan in Ferrers Lane near the Wicked Lady pub that night and if found might have proved useful witnesses.

At the inquest Detective Chief Superintendent Ron Harvey, in charge of the investigation, said that there were signs of a fierce struggle in Janie's car, and food that she had bought was scattered in gardens nearby. So far, police had not been able to establish where the murder had taken place, but considered it had been somewhere where the soil was chalky, in view of the muddy state of her car, and thought that her missing clothes might have been used to help free the car after it got bogged down in mud.

Police records showed that just half a mile from where Janie's car had been found abandoned, a young woman had been attacked and raped in her own car in July 1976. She had been seriously hurt, but managed to drive herself to hospital, and later gave police a good description of her attacker, a young black man with a scar on his face who told her he hated white women.

David Lashley, born in Barbados, had been recently released from prison on parole after serving part of a 12 year sentence for previous rapes, but had not been involved in the search for the July 1976 attacker, as his records made no mention of a facial scar. However, he was one of several convicted rapists seen by police after Janie Shepherd's murder, and his scar attracted police attention.

At an identity parade, the victim of the July 1976 attack identified him and in December 1977 he faced trial on an attempted murder and rape charge and was found guilty and sentenced to 18 years imprisonment.

Over the years the file on Janie Shepherd's unsolved murder remained open, and in 1988 Detective Superintendent Ian Whinnett of St Albans CID, not previously involved in the case, gave the details fresh consideration after Janie's mother, Mrs Angela Darling, wrote from Australia enquiring about the progress of the investigation.

He felt that new forensic techniques which had now been introduced might be able to throw a fresh light on the case. Then a significant breakthrough came shortly before Lashley was due for release from prison in 1989. He had struck up a friendship with another prisoner also serving a sentence for rape. Both were fitness fanatics keen on weight training, and while they were discussing a recent rape case Lashley confided how he had abducted a young woman at knife-point, slashed the sunroof of her car and raped and murdered her. He made it clear that he was bent on more revenge against women when he was released, and his listener decided to tell the authorities.

When Lashley emerged from Frankland Prison on 7th February 1989, the police were waiting and immediately arrested him and charged him with Janie Shepherd's murder. Lashley had apparently made no secret of his crime and other prison inmates came forward to report his boast of killing a young woman and dumping her body in woodland.

A year later and 13 years after Janie's death, David Lashley appeared at St Albans Crown Court charged with her murder. A semen stain on the back seat of Janie's car which it had been impossible to identify in 1977 was a vital piece of evidence, as DNA testing now available linked the stain to Lashley.

His choice of Nomansland Common to hide Janie's body may not have been entirely accidental. During the 1960s he and his wife had often been there when they visited his wife's son, who was a resident at the National Children's Home at Harpenden. And police believed he may often have driven across the Common while making calls in his van between St Albans and Harpenden. So perhaps on that dark, wet February night as he drove out of London with his tragic victim dead beside him, some memories of other times at Nomansland Common with his wife and child suggested that this might be a suitable place to hide the evidence of his horrible crime.

On 19th March 1990 David Lashley was found guilty and sentenced to life imprisonment. The Judge, Mr Justice Alliott, said, 'In my view you are such an appallingly dangerous man the real issue is whether the authorities can ever allow you your liberty in your natural life.' Now 50 years old, Lashley had spent most of his adult life in prison, his brief months of freedom a saga of brutal crimes. But this time the man once known as the Beast of Notting Hill, possessed of powerful strength and fitness acquired through obsessive weight training during his long spells of incarceration, returned to prison with little hope of ever regaining the freedom he had used to such evil effect.

HERTFORDSHIRE'S ROCK OF AGES

It looks like a huge petrified lump of the kind of old fashioned plum pudding that made Billy Bunter smile. And aptly enough, this pebble studded natural rock is called Hertfordshire puddingstone. Geologists know the ingredients, and the conditions which may have created it, but as in all good recipes, there is still, after 60 million years, an element of mystery.

Puddingstone can be bad news for a farmer whose farm machinery encounters a hidden lump, and in the past if heavy flooding or soil erosion brought puddingstones to light, they were superstitiously associated with the disaster and dubbed 'woestones'. And although stones usually turn up because of ploughing or the effects of hard frost or rain, there is some evidence that they do move very slowly towards the surface. Some years ago when the foundations of an old Buckinghamshire house became unstable, an enormous puddingstone was found to be gradually working its way through the kitchen floor!

Some people think puddingstone is lucky, and it has a reputation for warding off evil, hence another two names — hagstone or witchstone. Parish records of a burial in 1662 noted grimly 'that a hagstone be placed on the coffin for her bodie within be bewitched'. And yet another reason for putting a heavy puddingstone on a

The puddingstone at Kingsbury Mill.

new grave in the 18th century was to thwart body snatchers!

Although known as Hertfordshire puddingstone, to a lesser degree it can be found in Essex, Middlesex, Bedfordshire and Buckinghamshire. Extremely hard, it is what is geologically called a conglomerate, created around sixty million years ago when flint pebbles were bound together by a natural cement formed when water containing a silica solution penetrated the areas of sand and clay.

About 50 years ago Dr E.A. Rudge found a large puddingstone near Epping Forest which led him on a puddingstone hunt through Essex and Hertfordshire. He found about 130 of them, and was convinced he had discovered the markers of a Stone Age track to the prehistoric flint mining site of Grimes Graves in Norfolk, but this theory has been disputed by some archaeologists.

Chasing up some of the Doctor's finds in more recent years proved frustrating. Where was the boulder which Dr Rudge said had stood in New Kent Road, long before St

Albans? And others in Lattimore Road and by St Michael's Manor, St Albans proved to be just a memory.

However, tracing puddingstones throughout the county can be fascinating. One huge example stands outside Kingsbury Mill, St Albans and tradition says that the locals, fired by patriotism and strong ale, heaved it out of the Ver and set it there to commemorate Queen Victoria's Jubilee. More recently, a large find was made on the site of the new Seventh Day Adventist church at the top of Carlisle Avenue, St Albans. It took six men to lift it, and for some time it was on show in the grounds of the City Museum in Hatfield Road. Another huge boulder came to light during excavations for the Redbourn bypass and is still by the roadside near the roundabout at Harpenden Lane.

Many Hertfordshire churches have puddingstones in their foundation and walls and the reason for this may lie in a letter from Pope Gregory in AD 601 advising those bringing Christianity to Britain 'not to destroy the stones the heathens venerate' but to incorporate them in the churches being built. 'Thus', said the Pope, 'will the heathen more readily come to you.'

In Aldenham church not only does the 13th century tower contain puddingstones galore, but there is a remarkable tomb in the churchyard built in 1919 of the conglomerate. And in the grounds of Ashridge College there is a rockery made with many large puddingstones, and I understand the old ice house there is made of puddingstone, but this is not open to the public.

In the High Street at Standon there is a large puddingstone and on Standon Village Day, 1st May, among other celebrations the Standon Morris Men traditionally do their dawn dance at the Standon Puddingstone. When my family moved back to St Albans some years ago I was interested to find many large pieces of this unusual conglomerate in the garden rockery made by previous owners. A flint wall nearby had a large puddingstone boulder embedded in it,

The puddingstone tomb in Aldenham churchyard.

and I discovered that more than a hundred years ago the Herts Natural History Society recorded the discovery of a huge slab of puddingstone about 20 ft by 5 ft on the site of Townsend Farm where my house was built.

Puddingstone is exceptionally hard and in Roman times was used to produce hand querns for grinding grain, and some of these can be seen in the Verulamium Museum. It can also be cut and takes a high polish revealing the many beautiful colours of the pebbles, black, brown, red, yellow, pink and orange. Often used for jewellery and small items such as snuff boxes and ornaments in the 18th century, it is still valued by lapidarists.

Since earliest times myths and superstition have surrounded puddingstone, and it has many names such as breedingstone, growing stone, motherstone and angel stone, deriving from age-old beliefs that puddingstones can multiply, grow in size and magically attract other smaller pieces to themselves. They certainly have an effect on dowsing rods or pendulums. I conducted an unscientific experiment in my own garden and found that a pendulum held over various differently sized pieces of puddingstone rotated rapidly clockwise, but held over pieces of flint produced no reaction.

But whatever the truth about the mysterious powers and properties of puddingstone, it is a unique and beautiful natural feature of which Hertfordshire can be proud.

PETER THE WILD BOY

There are many intriguing reports over the centuries from various parts of the country about the mysterious arrival of apparently wild human beings whose origin is never satisfactorily explained.

Hertfordshire has its own wild man who first appeared in July 1724 in the woods near Hanover. He was described as a 'naked, brownish, black-haired creature, about twelve years old' who walked on all fours like an animal and seemed at home in the treetops. Britain's Hanoverian King, George I, heard about his capture and asked for him to be brought over to the English Court. Dean Swift wrote of the astonishment and interest caused by his arrival, and produced a pamphlet called *The Most Wonderful Wonder that ever appeared to the Wonder of the British Nation!*

But no attempts to encourage Peter the Wild Man to speak succeeded, and so when he proved less entertaining, he was sent to a farm in Hertfordshire in the care of Farmer James Fenn at Berkhamsted, who was paid £35 per annum.

There he quite happily roamed the countryside, and would stretch out in front of the fire at night like a large, amiable pet animal. Eventually his wanderings took him further afield and once he arrived in Norwich where he was imprisoned in the Bridewell. To keep tabs on him, James Fenn had a large collar made for Peter, which bore the words 'Peter the Wild Man from Hanover. Whoever will bring him

Peter the Wild Boy's collar photographed in the headmaster's study at Berkhamsted Collegiate School.

to Mr Fenn at Berkhamsted, Hertfordshire shall be paid for their trouble.'

Artist John Alefounder painted a miniature of Peter from life, depicting him at the age of about 73. At the church at Northchurch there is a brass plate with a sketch of Peter taken from Bartolozzi's engraving of the miniature. His collar still exists and is kept at Berkhamsted Collegiate School. Dr Paul G. Neeson, the Deputy Principal, kindly let me have a look and it proved to be smaller than I had expected. It is one inch deep and sixteen inches in circumference, and is made of leather inlaid with a brass band bearing the above words. The school also has an interesting engraving showing Peter in his middle years when his luxuriant hair and beard were black. The famous collar lies at his feet, so one would like to think he was allowed to remove it while relaxing peacefully at the farm.

I asked Dr Neeson how it was that these items were kept

at the school, and he said he understood that Peter had often visited the local alehouses, but the locals were inclined to tease and make fun of him and the school headmaster of those days would rescue Peter and take his tormentors to task. Dr Neeson thought this was probably the reason why these mementoes of Peter had come into the school's possession. Peter died on 22nd February 1785 and is buried near to the porch of St Mary's church, Northchurch, his origin and history as much a mystery as on the day he was found living wild in the Hanover woods.

DID JACK THE RIPPER KEEP A HERTFORDSHIRE PUB?

There are many unsolved mysteries in the history of crime but one in particular has exercised the minds of criminologists for more than a hundred years. Who was responsible for the series of savage murders that horrified London towards the end of the 19th century? The sadistically gruesome attacks upon women in the East End of the capital still arouse the same revulsion as they did when Victorians hurried home at night, fearful lest a dark shadow in a doorway or alley might suddenly materialise in the shape of Jack the Ripper.

In his memoirs Sir Melville Macnaghten, head of the CID, wrote, 'No-one who was living in London that autumn will forget the terror created by these murders. Even now I can recall the foggy evenings, and hear again the raucous cries of the newspaper boys: "Another horrible murder ..."'

In the squalid, vice-ridden East End of London work was hard to find and for many destitute women the only hope of getting enough money to live on was by prostitution. Mary Ann Nicholls, known as Polly, lived in a lodging house in Thrawl Street where a bug-ridden bed in a overcrowded room cost 4d a night, and apparently lacking the necessary money she had gone in search of a customer. It was 31st August 1888, and around 2.30 am she had a brief encounter with a friend. Less than an hour later, a man walking down Bucks Row, Whitechapel saw a woman apparently asleep on the ground. He gave her a friendly shake and found that, although she was still warm, Polly Nicholls was very dead indeed. Examination showed that her throat had been cut and her body horribly mutilated.

Prostitutes were often attacked in the slum areas of London, and at first Polly Nicholls' fate aroused little interest. But in the early morning of 8th September in a small backyard behind a barber's shop in Spitalfields market, a pathetic bundle proved to be what was left of Annie Chapman. It was a place often used by prostitutes, and she had been seen talking to a man described as about 5 ft 7 ins tall, with a moustache, dark clothes, hat and foreign accent. Shortly afterwards a man who went into the yard found her lying against a fence, her body mutilated by what must surely have been some kind of maniac.

London seethed with conjecture and fear of the inhuman monster who could commit such savagery. And then at the end of September 1888 there were two murders in one night. One was in the backyard of a club frequented by Russians, Poles and Jews, and another in Mitre Square in the city was discovered within the hour. A policeman patrolled the square every fifteen minutes or so, and when he passed through at around 1.30 am all was quiet, but at 1.45 am he came upon the body of Catherine Eddowes. Her murderer must have been close by as in a small passage leading out of the square there was obvious evidence that he had paused to wash the blood from his hands and maybe his weapon.

The Central News Agency had received several letters purporting to come from 'Your own light-hearted friend Jack the Ripper', and after the double murders on 30th September another letter announced that the next would be on 9th November.

At around 2 am that morning Mary Kelly, a young Irishwoman, 24 years old, was noticed talking to a dark, well dressed man with a heavy moustache, and they were seen entering the alleyway which led to her room in Miller's Court, off Dorset Street. Later that morning the landlord sent his assistant to collect the rent from No. 13. Mary Kelly, the occupant, was in arrears as usual and, getting no reply to his knock, the man put his hand through the broken window and drew aside the tattered curtain. The sight that met his eyes was indescribably horrible. Mary Kelly had been butchered, her remains gruesomely strewn around her dingy room.

Fear and suspicion reached fever pitch with the public, and several times police managed to prevent innocent citizens from being lynched in mistake for the Ripper. The description of the well dressed, dark moustached individual seen with Mary could fit many of the emigrants from Poland and Russia living in Whitechapel at that time and Inspector Abberline, who was working on the Ripper case, made enquiries at various immigrant clubs in the area, and at the barbers' shops where many Poles and Russians worked.

It was while visiting a shop in Whitechapel High Street that he first saw Severin Klosowski. Abberline was immediately struck by the Pole's resemblance to a man who had been arrested after the Ripper's second murder, but who had proved to be innocent. Klosowski was of medium height, dark with a heavy moustache. The Inspector called back again later, but Klosowski had gone, and it was weeks before he traced him again to another barber's in Tottenham.

Enquiries revealed that Klosowski was born in Poland in 1865 and at the age of 15 his parents had apprenticed him to a surgeon. He became what was called a junior surgeon in the Russian Army. Sometime in 1888 he had come to London, where he was continually on the move, working in different barbers' shops in the East End.

In spite of his rather brutal appearance he had a considerable appeal for women and at one time shared a ménage à trois with two women who were both devoted to him. But Inspector Abberline was unable to find out much about Klosowski — or any evidence to connect him with the Ripper murders.

Theories about Jack's identity abounded, as they have done ever since, and many people suspected even their nearest and dearest if they happened to be of middle height, moustached and given to unexplained absences at night. After the Mary Kelly atrocity nothing more was heard of the Ripper's activities for some time, and when a lawyer, Montague John Druitt, who had been under suspicion, was found dead in the Thames in the following January, the detectives on the case decided with relief that the Ripper's reign of terror was at an end. But there was no real evidence to connect Druitt with the murders.

One of the most persistent and extraordinary theories involved Queen Victoria's grandson, the Duke of Clarence. But the Duke who died in 1892 was at Sandringham celebrating his father's birthday on the day of the Kelly murder. But yet another theory involving the Duke claimed that he had a secret love child, and the baby's nanny had been Mary Kelly! She had told her prostitute friends in Whitechapel and Sir William Gull, Queen Victoria's physician, was delegated to silence them! The fact that Sir William had a stroke a year before the murders made him an unlikely suspect, and Joseph Sickert, son of the painter Walter Sickert, later admitted that his Jack the Ripper story was a hoax, although he still insisted that the Duke had fathered a daughter who had later married his friend, Walter, and that he, Joseph, was the result!

Meanwhile, what of Severin Klosowski? Late in 1889 he married a Polish girl, Lucy Baderski, and in 1890 they went to America to live in Jersey City. Ripper-type murders were reported from Jersey City and the Chief of the New York police consulted Scotland Yard. In February 1891 Lucy returned to Britain and later claimed that her husband had tried to kill her.

Severin Klosowski also returned to Britain where he lived for a time with a woman called Annie Chapman, and began to call himself George Chapman. His next alliance was with Isabella Spink, and in 1895 they announced they were married, and together ran a hairdresser's shop in Hastings. But the shop was not a success and before long the restless Chapman became licensee of a beerhouse in Bartholomew Square, London.

But Isabella was ailing; she became thin and was often sick. George Chapman was a model husband, looking after her assiduously and insisting on preparing her food and drink, and administering her medicine himself, telling friends that he was 'a bit of a doctor'. However, in spite of his care, Isabella died at Christmas 1897.

Chapman was not lonely for long. In August 1898, with Bessie Taylor as the new Mrs Chapman, they moved to the Grapes public house at Bishops Stortford. A friend of Bessie's who visited them at the Grapes found her unwell and on the point of going into hospital. After her return home Chapman's attitude changed and he became unkind, once threatening her with a revolver. They returned to London, but Bessie was ailing with frequent sickness and stomach pains. Again Chapman carefully nursed his wife, but Bessie died in February 1901.

Chapman's next matrimonial adventure was in the same year. He engaged an attractive barmaid, Maud Marsh, and within a short time she announced to her family that she and George had been quietly married. But from being a lively young girl, Maud changed and her poor health led to a spell in hospital where she soon recovered. But after her return home, her health rapidly deteriorated. By a strange coincidence her doctor was the same one who had attended the previous Mrs Chapman. He was puzzled by Maud's illness, and why in spite of treatment she grew steadily worse. Her husband gave her brandy, which made her vomit, and on one occasion when

The Grapes at Bishops Stortford, circa 1925. (Courtesy of W. Wright, Bishops Stortford Local History Museum)

Maud's mother finished off her brandy, she too was very sick.

Maud's mother had always had reservations about her daughter's husband, and privately suspected that there never had been any marriage. She called in her own doctor who at once suspected poison and alerted Maud's doctor. But it was too late to save Maud, who became much worse and died very suddenly. The doctor refused a death certificate, and a post mortem revealed the presence of poison. Chapman, on the point of flight with a ticket for Antwerp and a large wad of bank notes, was arrested on Coronation Day 1902 and a search of his papers revealed that in spite of his protests that he was George Chapman, an American citizen, he was really Severin Klosowski. Inspector Abberline, who had never forgotten Klosowski, said when he was arrested, 'You've got Jack the Ripper at last!'

It was proved that Chapman's three wives all died from antimony poisoning, and he was duly tried and executed. In Abberline's view, Chapman turned to poisoning when he found his career as the Ripper was becoming too risky. Whether or not the grim murders ascribed to Jack the Ripper were Chapman's doing may never be settled. It is certainly true that he looked the part, he was in the right places at the right time and he had surgical skill and a sadistic temperament.

As he stood behind the bar of the Grapes in Bishops Stortford, Hertfordshire, did he ever recall the dark alleys of Whitechapel a few years earlier when a meeting with a well dressed stranger could mean death? Did he share the revulsion of his fellow Eastenders at the memory, or did George Chapman cherish an appalling secret? Was George Chapman — or Severin Klosowski — really Jack the Ripper? Was Jack the Ripper ever a Hertfordshire publican? We shall probably never know ...